Soul on Ice

SOUL ON ICE

by *Eldridge Cleaver*

With an Introduction by Maxwell Geismar

▲ A DELTA BOOK

To Beverly, with whom I share
the ultimate of love

A DELTA BOOK
Published by
Dell Publishing Co., Inc.
750 Third Avenue, New York, N.Y. 10017
Copyright © 1968 by Eldridge Cleaver
Delta ® TM 755118, Dell Publishing Co., Inc.
A RAMPARTS BOOK reprinted by arrangement with
McGraw-Hill Book Company, New York
Manufactured in the United States of America
Ninth Printing

Acknowledgment is made to the following sources for permission to
quote from material already published:
The Dead Lecturer by LeRoi Jones. Copyright © 1964 by LeRoi Jones.
Reprinted by permission of The Sterling Lord Agency.
The Natural Superiority of Women by Ashley Montagu. Reprinted with
permission of The Macmillan Company. Copyright © 1953 by
Ashley Montagu.
"My Negro Problem—And Ours," *Commentary* by Norman Podhoretz.
Permission the author, copyright © February, 1963, by Norman
Podhoretz.
Commentary, from a letter by Irving Louis Horowitz. Reprinted by
permission of *Commentary*. Copyright © June, 1963, by the Amer-
ican Jewish Committee.
The Presidential Papers by Norman Mailer. Reprinted by permission
G. P. Putnam's Sons. Copyright © 1959 by Norman Mailer.
The Fire Next Time by James Baldwin. Reprinted with permission of
The Dial Press, Inc. Copyright © 1963, 1962 by James Baldwin.
On the Road by Jack Kerouac. Copyright © 1955, 1957 by Jack
Kerouac. Reprinted by permission of The Viking Press, Inc.
" 'Christ' and His Teachings" was first published in *Esquire* magazine
in April, 1967, as "The Guru of San Quentin."

Of all the beautiful people who have been so helpful in getting these writings into print, I'd like to thank especially Edward M. Keating, creator of *Ramparts* magazine, who was the first professional to pay any attention to my writings; Maxwell Geismar, whose criticism has helped me gain a degree of control over my materials; and David Welsh, for his invaluable assistance as an editor.

Contents

Introduction

by Maxwell Geismar

This book, written in prison by a young black American (or Afro-American), is one of the discoveries of the 1960s. In a literary epoch marked by a prevailing mediocrity of expression, a lack of substantial new talent, a kind of spiritual slough after the great wave of American writing from the 1920s to the 1940s, Eldridge Cleaver's is one of the distinctive new literary voices to be heard. It reminds me of the great days of the past. It has echoes of Richard Wright's *Native Son,* just as its true moral affinity is with one of the few other fine books of our period, the *Autobiography of Malcolm X,* and as it represents in American terms the only comparable approach to the writings of Frantz Fanon.

In a curious way Cleaver's book has definite parallels with Fanon's *Black Skin White Masks.* In both books the central problem is of *identification* as a black soul which has been "colonized"—more subtly perhaps in the United States for some three hundred years, but perhaps even more pervasively—by an oppressive white society that projects its brief, narrow vision of life as eternal truth. Eldridge Cleaver very fittingly opens these Letters from Prison with the section called "On Becoming" in 1954, when he was eighteen years old. The Supreme Court had just outlawed segregation; he was in Folsom Prison, California, on a marijuana charge; he would be sent back to prison again for what he describes as rape-on-principle. There is a kind of adolescent innocence—the innocence of genius—in these early letters, just as later there is savage irony and a profound deadpan humor about the white man's civilization in the twentieth-century United States.

Cleaver is simply one of the best cultural critics now writing, and I include in this statement both the formal sociologists and those contemporary fictionists who have mainly abandoned this province of literature for the cultivation of the cult of sensibility. (I am aware also of what may be considered excessive praise in this introduction; in that case I can only beg the reader to stop reading me and start directly with Cleaver.) As in Malcolm X's case, here is an "outside" critic who takes pleasure in dissecting the deepest and most cherished notions of our personal and social behavior; and it takes a certain amount of courage and a "willed objectivity" to read him. He rakes our favorite prejudices with the savage claws of his prose until our wounds are bare, our psyche is exposed, and we must either fight back or laugh with him for the service he has done us. For the "souls of black folk," in W. E. B. Du Bois' phrase, are the best mirror in which to see the white American self in mid-twentieth century.

It takes a certain boldness on Cleaver's part, also, to open this collection of essays with the section not merely on rape but on the whole profound relationship of black men and white women. There is a secret kind of sexual mysticism in this writer which adds depth and tone to his social commentary; this is a highly literary and imaginative mind surveying the salient aspects of our common life. There follow the Four Vignettes—on Watts, on the Muslims, on Catholicism and Thomas Merton, and on the heroic prison teacher called Lovdjieff. Here we begin to feel the reach and depth of Eldridge Cleaver's mind on emotional and philosophical issues as well as historical and social ones—and yes, "heroic," a note barely sounded in contemporary fiction, is not inappropriate for certain parts of this deeply revolutionary collection of essays.

After a series of religious experiences in prison, the young Cleaver became a Muslim convert, then a Muslim preacher of extraordinary eloquence and conviction, and then a firm follower of Malcom X. Through this process he regained his previously alienated and splintered self-image as a child of the California black ghetto; and from this point began the remarkable process of self-analysis, self-education and self-expression described in the pages of this book. The essay called "Initial Reactions on the Assassination of Malcolm X," written in 1965, is a document of prime importance for an understanding of the outcast black American soul today; it illuminates all the long hot summers of rioting, violence, and "senseless" destruction.

Here Cleaver unites the militant black resistance movement in the United States with the currents of world revolution in a way which may come as a shock to many white Americans of liberal persuasion and spiritual good-will. Yet it is so, and the sooner we try to understand it the better, and Eldridge Cleaver can help us in this process. "We shall have our manhood. We shall have it or the earth will be leveled by our attempts to gain it"—and some parts of the American earth have already been leveled by this prophetic spirit of wrath—and human dignity. But it is the part of the book called "Blood of the Beast," and such pieces as "The White Race and Its Heroes," that I find of primary importance, and of the greatest literary value. Describing himself as an "Ofay Watcher," Cleaver describes this historical period and this American culture in terms of the most astringent accuracy, the most ruthless irony, and the most insistent truthfulness. He reminds us of all the simple verities that decades of Cold War distortion and hypocrisy have almost wiped from our historical record —our historical consciousness.

The book is a handsome account of those years in the early sixties when the Civil Rights campaign stirred up a national psyche that had been unnaturally comatose, slothful, and evasive since the McCarthyite trauma. There is an atmosphere of turbulence in these essays, moving from the advent of the Beats and Jack Kerouac's *On The Road* to LeRoi Jones' revolutionary verses and then back to the Abolitionists (so scorned and despised by the Southern revisionist historians of the modern epoch), to Harriet Beecher Stowe and to that famous Fourth of July peroration for the slave race by Frederick Douglass in 1852.

In the concluding part of this book it seems that Eldridge Cleaver has reached his own spiritual convalescence, his healed spirit (no longer racist or narrowly nationalist), and his mature power as a writer—and how those pages do sparkle! The essay "Lazarus, Come Forth," on Negro celebrities and on boxing as the virility symbol of the American masses, and on Muhammad Ali in particular, is a beauty. Here Cleaver begins to touch on all aspects of American culture with a sure touch and a clear vision. "Notes on a Native Son" is the best analysis of James Baldwin's literary career I have read; and while Cleaver calmly says things that no white critic could really dare to say, there is not a trace of petty artistic jealousy or self-vanity in his discussion—such as that, for example, which marked Baldwin's own repudiation of his former mentor, Richard Wright. The essay called "Rallying Round the Flag" gives us the plain, hard, truthful Afro-American view of the Vietnam war which Martin Luther King, just

lately, has corroborated—it is in fact the world view of
our aberrant national behavior in southeast Asia. But just
as this volume opens on the theme of love, just as Eldridge
Cleaver never misses the sexual core of every social (or
racial) phenomenon, so it closes on it.

There are touching and illuminating letters to the California civil-rights lawyer Beverly Axelrod, who, awed by
Cleaver's talent as all of us were who first encountered
it several years ago, succeeded in obtaining his release
from Folsom Prison after nine years. There is the section
of the book called "The Primeval Mitosis," close to a kind
of Laurentian sexual mysticism again, which bodies forth
such engaging social types as the Supermasculine Menial
and the Ultrafeminine Doll: the sexual-social myth Cleaver
has invented for the second-class black male (all body, no
brain) and the pure white Southern lady, say, languishing
and swooning her days away. These are the exotic myths
and fabricated legends of a racial caste system embodied
in a hypocritical class society. These are the satiric fan-
tasies hovering around something which might be called
the "essential miscegenation" as the missing key, the unthinkable solution to the American race problem.

I had forgotten to mention the wonderfully ironic de-
scriptions of the Twist as the social symptom of the new
age of dawning racial equality. Here, as with the Beatles
and Rock n' Roll, when Eldridge Cleaver moves into the
area of mass entertainment in the United States, he is as
close as he ever comes to an open laughter at the white
man's antics; just as in the concluding apostrophe from
the Black Eunuch to the Black Queen—to the fertile black
womb of all history—he reminds us how civilization has
always mocked human gaiety.   M.G.

Harrison, New York

June 1967

I: Letters From Prison

On Becoming

Folsom Prison
June 25, 1965

Nineteen fifty-four, when I was eighteen years old, is held to be a crucial turning point in the history of the Afro-American—for the U.S.A. as a whole—the year segregation was outlawed by the U.S. Supreme Court. It was also a crucial year for me because on June 18, 1954, I began serving a sentence in state prison for possession of marijuana.

The Supreme Court decision was only one month old when I entered prison, and I do not believe that I had even the vaguest idea of its importance or historical significance. But later, the acrimonious controversy ignited by the end of the separate-but-equal doctrine was to have a profound effect on me. This controversy awakened me to my position in America and I began to form a concept of what it meant to be black in white America.

Of course I'd always known that I was black, but I'd never really stopped to take stock of what I was involved in. I met life as an individual and took my chances. Prior to 1954, we lived in an atmosphere of novocain. Negroes found it necessary, in order to maintain whatever sanity they could, to remain somewhat aloof and detached from "the problem." We accepted indignities and the mechanics of the apparatus of oppression without reacting by sitting-in

3

or holding mass demonstrations. Nurtured by the fires of the controversy over segregation, I was soon aflame with indignation over my newly discovered social status, and inwardly I turned away from America with horror, disgust and outrage.

In Soledad state prison, I fell in with a group of young blacks who, like myself, were in vociferous rebellion against what we perceived as a continuation of slavery on a higher plane. We cursed everything American—including baseball and hot dogs. All respect we may have had for politicians, preachers, lawyers, governors, Presidents, senators, congressmen was utterly destroyed as we watched them temporizing and compromising over right and wrong, over legality and illegality, over constitutionality and unconstitutionality. We knew that in the end what they were clashing over was us, what to do with the blacks, and whether or not to start treating us as human beings. I despised all of them.

The segregationists were condemned out of hand, without even listening to their lofty, finely woven arguments. The others I despised for wasting time in debates with the segregationists: why not just crush them, put them in prison —they were defying the law, weren't they? I defied the law and they put me in prison. So why not put those dirty mothers in prison too? I had gotten caught with a shopping bag full of marijuana, a shopping bag full of love—I was in love with the weed and I did not for one minute think that anything was wrong with getting high. I had been getting high for four or five years and was convinced, with the zeal of a crusader, that marijuana was superior to lush—yet the rulers of the land seemed all to be lushes. I could not see how they were more justified in drinking than I was in blowing the gage. I was a grasshopper, and it was natural that I felt myself to be unjustly imprisoned.

While all this was going on, our group was espousing

atheism. Unsophisticated and not based on any philosophical rationale, our atheism was pragmatic. I had come to believe that there is no God; if there is, men do not know anything about him. Therefore, all religions were phony—which made all preachers and priests, in our eyes, fakers, including the ones scurrying around the prison who, curiously, could put in a good word for you with the Almighty Creator of the universe but could not get anything down with the warden or parole board—they could usher you through the Pearly Gates *after you were dead,* but not through the prison gate *while you were still alive and kicking.* Besides, men of the cloth who work in prison have an ineradicable stigma attached to them in the eyes of convicts because they escort condemned men into the gas chamber. Such men of God are powerful arguments in favor of atheism. Our atheism was a source of enormous pride to me. Later on, I bolstered our arguments by reading Thomas Paine and his devastating critique of Christianity in particular and organized religion in general.

Through reading I was amazed to discover how confused people were. I had thought that, out there beyond the horizon of my own ignorance, unanimity existed, that even though I myself didn't know what was happening in the universe, other people certainly did. Yet here I was discovering that the whole U.S.A. was in a chaos of disagreement over segregation/integration. In these circumstances I decided that the only safe thing for me to do was go for myself. It became clear that it was possible for me to take the initiative: instead of simply *reacting* I could *act.* I could unilaterally—whether anyone agreed with me or not—repudiate all allegiances, morals, values—even while continuing to exist within this society. My mind would be free and no power in the universe could force me to accept something if I didn't want to. But I would take my own sweet time. That, too, was a part of my new freedom. I would accept nothing until it was proved that it was good—for me. I became an extreme iconoclast. Any affirmative assertion made by anyone around me became a target for tirades of criticism and denunciation.

This little game got good to me and I got good at it. I attacked all forms of piety, loyalty, and sentiment: marriage, love, God, patriotism, the Constitution, the founding fathers, law, concepts of right-wrong-good-evil, all forms of ritualized and conventional behavior. As I pranced about, club in hand, seeking new idols to smash, I encountered really for the first time in my life, with any seriousness, The Ogre, rising up before me in a mist. I discovered, with alarm, that The Ogre possessed a tremendous and dreadful power over me, and I didn't understand this power or why I was at its mercy. I tried to repudiate The Ogre, root it out of my heart as I had done God, Constitution, principles, morals, and values—but The Ogre had its claws buried in the core of my being and refused to let go. I fought frantically to be free, but The Ogre only mocked me and sank its claws deeper into my soul. I knew then that I had found an important key, that if I conquered The Ogre and broke its power over me I would be free. But I also knew that it was a race against time and that if I did not win I would certainly be broken and destroyed. I, a black man, confronted The Ogre—the white woman.

In prison, those things withheld from and denied to the prisoner become precisely what he wants most of all, of course. Because we were locked up in our cells before darkness fell, I used to lie awake at night racked by painful craving to take a leisurely stroll under the stars, or to go to the beach, to drive a car on a freeway, to grow a beard, or to make love to a woman.

Since I was not married conjugal visits would not have

solved my problem. I therefore denounced the idea of conjugal visits as inherently unfair; single prisoners needed and deserved *action* just as married prisoners did. I advocated establishing a system under Civil Service whereby salaried women would minister to the needs of those prisoners who maintained a record of good behavior. If a married prisoner preferred his own wife, that would be his right. Since California was not about to inaugurate either conjugal visits or the Civil Service, one could advocate either with equal enthusiasm and with the same result: nothing.

This may appear ridiculous to some people. But it was very real to me and as urgent as the need to breathe, because I was in my bull stage and lack of access to females was absolutely a form of torture. I suffered. My mistress at the time of my arrest, the beautiful and lonely wife of a serviceman stationed overseas, died unexpectedly three weeks after I entered prison; and the rigid, dehumanized rules governing correspondence between prisoners and free people prevented me from corresponding with other young ladies I knew. It left me without any contact with females except those in my family.

In the process of enduring my confinement, I decided to get myself a pin-up girl to paste on the wall of my cell. I would fall in love with her and lavish my affections upon her. She, a symbolic representative of the forbidden tribe of women, would sustain me until I was free. Out of the center of *Esquire,* I married a voluptuous bride. Our marriage went along swell for a time: no quarrels, no complaints. And then, one evening when I came in from school, I was shocked and enraged to find that the guard had entered my cell, ripped my sugar from the wall, torn her into little pieces, and left the pieces floating in the commode: it was like seeing a dead body floating in a lake.

Giving her a proper burial, I flushed the commode. As the saying goes, I sent her to Long Beach. But I was genuinely beside myself with anger: almost every cell, excepting those of the homosexuals, had a pin-up girl on the wall and the guards didn't bother them. Why, I asked the guard the next day, had he singled me out for special treatment?

"Don't you know we have a rule against pasting up pictures on the walls?" he asked me.

"Later for the rules," I said. "You know as well as I do that that rule is not enforced."

"Tell you what," he said, smiling at me (the smile put me on my guard), "I'll compromise with you: get yourself a colored girl for a pinup—no white women—and I'll let it stay up. Is that a deal?"

I was more embarrassed than shocked. He was laughing in my face. I called him two or three dirty names and walked away. I can still recall his big moon-face, grinning at me over yellow teeth. The disturbing part about the whole incident was that a terrible feeling of guilt came over me as I realized that I had chosen the picture of the white girl over the available pictures of black girls. I tried to rationalize it away, but I was fascinated by the truth involved. Why hadn't I thought about it in this light before? So I took hold of the question and began to inquire into my feelings. Was it true, did I really prefer white girls over black? The conclusion was clear and inescapable: I did. I decided to check out my friends on this point and it was easy to determine, from listening to their general conversation, that the white woman occupied a peculiarly prominent place in all of our frames of reference. With what I have learned since then, this all seems terribly elementary now. But at the time, it was a tremendously intriguing adventure of discovery.

One afternoon, when a large group of Negroes was on

the prison yard shooting the breeze, I grabbed the floor and posed the question: which did they prefer, white women or black? Some said Japanese women were their favorite, others said Chinese, some said European women, others said Mexican women—they all stated a preference, and they generally freely admitted their dislike for black women.

"I don't want nothing black but a Cadillac," said one.

"If money was black I wouldn't want none of it," put in another.

A short little stud, who was a very good lightweight boxer with a little man's complex that made him love to box heavyweights, jumped to his feet. He had a yellowish complexion and we called him Butterfly.

"All you niggers are sick!" Butterfly spat out. "I don't like no stinking white woman. My grandma is a white woman and I don't even like her!"

But it just so happened that Butterfly's crime partner was in the crowd, and after Butterfly had his say, his crime partner said, "Aw, sit on down and quit that lying, lil o' chump. What about that gray girl in San Jose who had your nose wide open? Did you like her, or were you just running after her with your tongue hanging out of your head because you hated her?"

Partly because he was embarrassed and partly because his crime partner was a heavyweight, Butterfly flew into him. And before we could separate them and disperse, so the guard would not know who had been fighting, Butterfly bloodied his crime partner's nose. Butterfly got away but, because of the blood, his crime partner got caught. I ate dinner with Butterfly that evening and questioned him sharply about his attitude toward white women. And after an initial evasiveness he admitted that the white woman bugged him too. "It's a sickness," he said. "All our lives we've had the white woman dangled before our eyes like a carrot on a stick before a donkey: look but don't touch." (In 1958, after I had gone out on parole and was returned to San Quentin as a parole violater with a new charge, Butterfly was still there. He had become a Black Muslim and was chiefly responsible for teaching me the Black Muslim philosophy. Upon his release from San Quentin, Butterfly joined the Los Angeles Mosque, advanced rapidly through the ranks, and is now a full-fledged minister of one of Elijah Muhammad's mosques in another city. He successfully completed his parole, got married—to a very black girl—and is doing fine.)

From our discussion, which began that evening and has never yet ended, we went on to notice how thoroughly, as a matter of course, a black growing up in America is indoctrinated with the white race's standard of beauty. Not that the whites made a conscious, calculated effort to do this, we thought, but since they constituted the majority the whites brainwashed the blacks by the very processes the whites employed to indoctrinate themselves with their own group standards. It intensified my frustrations to know that I was indoctrinated to see the white woman as more beautiful and desirable than my own black woman. It drove me into books seeking light on the subject. In Richard Wright's *Native Son,* I found Bigger Thomas and a keen insight into the problem.

My interest in this area persisted undiminished and then, in 1955, an event took place in Mississippi which turned me inside out: Emmett Till, a young Negro down from Chicago on a visit, was murdered, allegedly for flirting with a white woman. He had been shot, his head crushed from repeated blows with a blunt instrument, and his badly decomposed body was recovered from the river with a heavy weight on it. I was, of course, angry over the whole bit, but one day I saw in a magazine a picture of the white woman with whom Emmett Till was said to have flirted. While looking at the picture, I felt that little tension in the center of my chest I experience when a woman appeals to me. I was disgusted and angry with myself. Here was a woman who had caused the death of a black, possibly because, when he looked at her, he also felt the same tensions of lust and desire in his chest—and probably for the same general reasons that I felt them. It was all unacceptable to me. I looked at the picture again and again, and in spite of everything and against my will and the hate I felt for the woman and all that she represented, she appealed to me. I flew into a rage at myself, at America, at white women, at the history that had placed those tensions of lust and desire in my chest.

Two days later, I had a "nervous breakdown." For several days I ranted and raved against the white race, against white women in particular, against white America in general. When I came to myself, I was locked in a padded cell with not even the vaguest memory of how I got there. All I could recall was an eternity of pacing back and forth in the cell, preaching to the unhearing walls.

I had several sessions with a psychiatrist. His conclusion was that I hated my mother. How he arrived at this conclusion I'll never know, because he knew nothing about my mother; and when he'd ask me questions I would answer him with absurd lies. What revolted me about him was that he had heard me denouncing the whites, yet each time he interviewed me he deliberately guided the conversation back to my family life, to my childhood. That in itself was all right, but he deliberately blocked all my attempts to bring out the racial question, and he made it clear that he was not interested in my attitude toward whites. This was a Pandora's box he did not care to open. After I ceased my diatribes against the whites, I was let out of the hospital, back into the general inmate population just as if nothing had happened. I continued to brood over these events and over the dynamics of race relations in America.

During this period I was concentrating my reading in the field of economics. Having previously dabbled in the theories and writings of Rousseau, Thomas Paine, and Voltaire, I had added a little polish to my iconoclastic stance, without, however, bothering too much to understand their affirmative positions. In economics, because everybody seemed to find it necessary to attack and condemn Karl Marx in their writings, I sought out his books, and although he kept me with a headache, I took him for my authority. I was not prepared to understand him, but I was able to see in him a thoroughgoing critique and condemnation of capitalism. It was like taking medicine for me to find that, indeed, American capitalism deserved all the hatred and contempt that I felt for it in my heart. This had a positive, stabilizing effect upon me—to an extent because I was not about to become stable—and it diverted me from my previous preoccupation: morbid broodings on the black man and the white woman. Pursuing my readings into the history of socialism, I read, with very little understanding, some of the passionate, exhortatory writings of Lenin; and I fell in love with Bakunin and Nechayev's *Catechism of the Revolutionist*—the principles of which, along with some of Machiavelli's advice, I sought to incorporate into my own behavior. I took the *Catechism* for my bible and, standing on a one-man platform that had nothing to do with the reconstruction of society, I began consciously incorporating these principles into my daily life, to employ tactics of ruthlessness in my dealings with everyone with whom I came into contact. And I began to look at white America through these new eyes.

Somehow I arrived at the conclusion that, as a matter of principle, it was of paramount importance for me to have an antagonistic, ruthless attitude toward white women. The term *outlaw* appealed to me and at the time my parole date was drawing near, I considered myself to be mentally free—I was an "outlaw." I had stepped outside of the white man's law, which I repudiated with scorn and self-satisfaction. I became a law unto myself—my own legislature, my own supreme court, my own executive. At the moment I walked out of the prison gate, my feelings toward white women in general could be summed up in the following lines:

TO A WHITE GIRL

*I love you
Because you're white,
Not because you're charming
Or bright.
Your whiteness
Is a silky thread
Snaking through my thoughts
In redhot patterns
Of lust and desire.*

*I hate you
Because you're white.
Your white meat
Is nightmare food.
White is
The skin of Evil.
You're my Moby Dick,
White Witch,
Symbol of the rope and hanging tree,
Of the burning cross.*

Loving you thus
And hating you so,
My heart is torn in two.
Crucified.

I became a rapist. To refine my technique and *modus operandi*, I started out by practicing on black girls in the ghetto—in the black ghetto where dark and vicious deeds appear not as aberrations or deviations from the norm, but as part of the sufficiency of the Evil of a day—and when I considered myself smooth enough, I crossed the tracks and sought out white prey. I did this consciously, deliberately, willfully, methodically—though looking back I see that I was in a frantic, wild, and completely abandoned frame of mind.

Rape was an insurrectionary act. It delighted me that I was defying and trampling upon the white man's law, upon his system of values, and that I was defiling his women—and this point, I believe, was the most satisfying to me because I was very resentful over the historical fact of how the white man has used the black woman. I felt I was getting revenge. From the site of the act of rape, consternation spreads outwardly in concentric circles. I wanted to send waves of consternation throughout the white race. Recently, I came upon a quotation from one of LeRoi Jones' poems, taken from his book *The Dead Lecturer:*

A cult of death need of the simple striking arm under the street lamp. The cutters from under their rented earth. Come up, black dada nihilismus. Rape the white girls. Rape their fathers. Cut the mothers' throats.

I have lived those lines and I know that if I had not been apprehended I would have slit some white throats. There are, of course, many young blacks out there right now who are slitting white throats and raping the white girl. They are not doing this because they read LeRoi Jones' poetry, as some of his critics seem to believe. Rather, LeRoi is expressing the funky facts of life.

After I returned to prison, I took a long look at myself and, for the first time in my life, admitted that I was wrong, that I had gone astray—astray not so much from the white man's law as from being human, civilized—for I could not approve the act of rape. Even though I had some insight into my own motivations, I did not feel justified. I lost my self-respect. My pride as a man dissolved and my whole fragile moral structure seemed to collapse, completely shattered.

That is why I started to write. To save myself.

I realized that no one could save me but myself. The prison authorities were both uninterested and unable to help me. I had to seek out the truth and unravel the snarled web of my motivations. I had to find out who I am and what I want to be, what type of man I should be, and what I could do to become the best of which I was capable. I understood that what had happened to me had also happened to countless other blacks and it would happen to many, many more.

I learned that I had been taking the easy way out, running away from problems. I also learned that it is easier to do evil than it is to do good. And I have been terribly impressed by the youth of America, black and white. I am proud of them because they have reaffirmed my faith in humanity. I have come to feel what must be love for the young people of America and I want to be part of the good and greatness that they want for all people. From my prison cell, I have watched America slowly coming awake. It is not fully awake yet, but there is soul in the air and everywhere I see beauty. I have watched the sit-ins, the freedom raids, the Mississippi Blood Summers, demonstrations all over the country, the FSM movement, the teach-ins, and the mounting protest over Lyndon Strangelove's foreign policy—all of this, the thousands of little details, show me it is time to straighten up and fly right. That is why I decided to concentrate on my writings and efforts in this area. We are a very sick country—I, perhaps, am sicker than most. But I accept that. I told you in the beginning that I am extremist by nature—so it is only right that I should be extremely sick.

I was very familiar with the Eldridge who came to prison, but that Eldridge no longer exists. And the one I am now is in some ways a stranger to me. You may find this difficult to understand but it is very easy for one in prison to lose his sense of self. And if he has been undergoing all kinds of extreme, involved, and unregulated changes, then he ends up not knowing who he is. Take the point of being attractive to women. You can easily see how a man can lose his arrogance or certainty on that point while in prison! When he's in the free world, he gets constant feedback on how he looks from the number of female heads he turns when he walks down the street. In prison he gets only hate-stares and sour frowns. Years and years of bitter looks. Individuality is not nourished in prison, neither by the officials nor by the convicts. It is a deep hole out of which to climb.

What must be done, I believe, is that all these problems —particularly the sickness between the white woman and the black man—must be brought out into the open, dealt with and resolved. I know that the black man's sick attitude toward the white woman is a revolutionary sickness: it keeps him perpetually out of harmony with the system that is oppressing him. Many whites flatter themselves with the idea that the Negro male's lust and desire for the white dream girl is purely an esthetic attraction, but nothing could be farther from the truth. His motivation is often of such a bloody, hateful, bitter, and malignant nature that whites would really be hard pressed to find it flattering. I have discussed these points with prisoners who were convicted of rape, and their motivations are very plain. But they are very reluctant to discuss these things with white men who, by and large, make up the prison staffs. I believe that in the experience of these men lies the knowledge and wisdom that must be utilized to help other youngsters who are heading in the same direction. I think all of us, the entire nation, will be better off if we bring it all out front. A lot of people's feelings will be hurt, but that is the price that must be paid.

It may be that I can harm myself by speaking frankly and directly, but I do not care about that at all. Of course I want to get out of prison, badly, but I shall get out some day. I am more concerned with what I am going to be after I get out. I know that by following the course which I have charted I will find my salvation. If I had followed the path laid down for me by the officials, I'd undoubtedly have long since been out of prison—but I'd be less of a man. I'd be weaker and less certain of where I want to go, what I want to do, and how to go about it.

The price of hating other human beings is loving oneself less.

Soul on Ice

Folsom Prison
October 9, 1965

I'm perfectly aware that I'm in prison, that I'm a Negro, that I've been a rapist, and that I have a Higher Uneducation. I never know what significance I'm supposed to attach to these factors. But I have a suspicion that, because of these aspects of my character, "free-normal-educated" people rather expect me to be more reserved, penitent, remorseful, and not too quick to shoot off my mouth on certain subjects. But I let them down, disappoint them, make them gape at me in a sort of stupor, as if they're thinking: "You've got your nerve! Don't you realize that you owe a debt to society?" My answer to all such thoughts lurking in their split-level heads, crouching behind their squinting bombardier eyes, is that the blood of Vietnamese peasants has paid off all my debts; that the Vietnamese people, afflicted with a rampant disease called Yankees, through their sufferings—as opposed to the "frustration" of fat-assed American geeks safe at home worrying over whether to have bacon, ham, or sausage with their grade-A eggs in the morning, while Vietnamese worry each morning whether the Yankees will gas them, burn them up, or blow away their humble pads in a hail of bombs—have canceled all my IOUs.

In beginning this letter I could just as easily have mentioned other aspects of my situation; I could have said: I'm perfectly aware that I'm tall, that I'm skinny, that I need a shave, that I'm hard-up enough to suck my grandmother's old withered tits, and that I would dig (deeper than deeply) getting *clean* once more—not only in the steam-bath sense, but in getting sharp as an *Esquire* square with a Harlem touch—or that I would like to put on a pair of bib overalls and become a Snicker, or that I'd like to leap the whole last mile and grow a beard and don whatever threads the local nationalism might require and comrade with Che Guevara, and share his fate, blazing a new pathfinder's trail through the stymied upbeat brain of the New Left, or how I'd just love to be in Berkeley right now, to roll in that mud, frolic in that sty of funky revolution, to breathe in its heady fumes, and look with roving eyes for a new John Brown, Eugene Debs, a blacker-meaner-keener Malcolm X, a Robert Franklin Williams with less rabbit in his hot blood, an American Lenin, Fidel, a Mao-Mao, A MAO MAO, A MAO MAO, A MAO MAO, A MAO MAO, A MAO MAO, A MAO MAO. . . . All of which is true.

But what matters is that I have fallen in love with my lawyer! Is that surprising? A convict is expected to have a high regard for *anyone* who comes to his aid, who tries to help him and who expends time, energy, and money in an effort to set him free. But can a convict really love a lawyer? It goes against the grain. Convicts hate lawyers. To walk around a prison yard and speak well of a lawyer is to raise the downcast eyebrows of felons who've been bitten by members of the Bar and Grill. Convicts are convinced that lawyers must have a secret little black book which no one else is ever allowed to see, a book that schools lawyers in an esoteric morality in which the Highest Good is treachery and crossing one's dumb and trusting client the noblest of deeds. It was learned by the convicts that I'd gotten busted with some magazines given to me by my lawyer and that I was thrown in the Hole for it. Convicts smiled knowingly and told me that I had gone for the greasy pig, that my lawyer had set me up, and that if I couldn't see through the plot I was so stupid that I would buy not only the Golden Gate Bridge but some fried ice cream.

It was my turn to smile knowingly. A convict's paranoia is as thick as the prison wall—and just as necessary. Why should we have faith in anyone? Even our wives and lovers whose beds we have shared, with whom we have shared the tenderest moments and most delicate relations, leave us after a while, put us down, cut us clean aloose and treat us like they hate us, won't even write us a letter, send us a Christmas card every other year, or a quarter for a pack of cigarettes or a tube of toothpaste now and then. All society shows the convict its ass and expects him to kiss it: the convict feels like kicking it or putting a bullet in it. A convict sees man's fangs and claws and learns quickly to bare and unsheath his own, for real and final. To maintain a hold on the ideals and sentiments of civilization in such circumstances is probably impossible. How much more incredible is it, then, while rooted in this pit, to fall in love, and with a lawyer! Use a lawyer, yes: use anybody. Even tell the lawyer that you're in love. But you will always know when you are lying and even if you could manage to fool the lawyer you could never manage to fool yourself.

And why does it make you sad to see how everything hangs by such thin and whimsical threads? Because you're a dreamer, an incredible dreamer, with a tiny spark hidden somewhere inside you which cannot die, which even you cannot kill or quench and which tortures you horribly because all the odds are against its continual burning. In the midst of the foulest decay and putrid savagery, this spark speaks to you of beauty, of human warmth and kindness, of goodness, of greatness, of heroism, of martyrdom, and it speaks to you of love.

So I love my lawyer. My lawyer is not an ordinary person. My lawyer is a rebel, a revolutionary who is alienated fundamentally from the *status quo,* probably with as great an intensity, conviction, and irretrievability as I am alienated from it—and probably with more intelligence, compassion, and humanity. If you read the papers, you are no doubt aware of my lawyer's incessant involvement in agitation against all manifestations of the monstrous evil of our system, such as our intervention in the internal affairs of the Vietnamese people or the invasion of the Dominican Republic by U.S. Marines. And my lawyer defends civil rights demonstrators, sit-iners, and the Free Speech students who rebelled against the Kerr–Strong machine at the University of California. My love for my lawyer is due, in part, to these activities and involvements, because we are always on the same side of the issues. And I love all my allies. But this, which may be the beginning of an explanation, does not nearly explain what goes on between my lawyer and me.

I suppose that I should be honest and, before going any further, admit that my lawyer is a woman—or maybe I should have held back with that piece of the puzzle—a very excellent, unusual, and beautiful woman. I know that *she* believes that I do not really love her and that I am confusing a combination of lust and gratitude for love. Lust and gratitude I feel abundantly, but I also love this woman. And I fear that, believing that I do not love her, she will act according to that belief.

At night, I talk with her in my sleep, long dialogues in which she answers back. We alternate in speaking, like in the script of a play. And let me say that I don't believe a word she says. While we are talking, I participate and believe everything, taking her word as her bond. But when I awake, I repudiate the conversation and disbelieve her. I awake refreshed, and though my sleep has been restless, I am not tired. Except for a few lost hours in which she slips away and I fall into a deep sleep, I hover on a level between consciousness and peace, and the dialogue ensues. It does not bother me now. I have often gone through this when something seizes my mind.

I place a great deal of emphasis on people really listening to each other, to what the other person has to say, because you very seldom encounter a person who is capable of taking either you or himself seriously. Of course, when I was out of prison I was not really like this; the seeds were there, but there was too much confusion and madness mixed in. I had a profound desire for communicating with and getting to know other people, but I was incapable of doing so. I didn't know how.

Getting to know someone, entering that new world, is an ultimate, irretrievable leap into the unknown. The prospect is terrifying. The stakes are high. The emotions are overwhelming. The two people are reluctant really to strip themselves naked in front of each other, because in doing so they make themselves vulnerable and give enormous power over themselves one to the other. How often they inflict pain and torment upon each other! Better to maintain shallow, superficial affairs; that way the scars are not too deep. No blood is hacked from the soul.

But I do not believe a beautiful relationship has to end always in carnage, or that we have to be fraudulent and pretentious with one another. If we project fraudulent, pretentious images, or if we fantasize each other into distorted caricatures of what we really are, then, when we awake from the trance and see beyond the sham and front, all will dissolve, all will die or be transformed into bitterness and hate. I know that sometimes people fake on each other of genuine motives to hold onto the object of their tend feelings. They see themselves as so inadequate that they feel forced to wear a mask in order continuously to impress the second party.

If a man is free—not in prison, the Army, a monastery, hospital, spaceship, submarine—and living a normal life with the usual multiplicity of social relations with individuals of both sexes, it may be that he is incapable of experiencing the total impact of another individual upon himself. The competing influences and conflicting forces of other personalities may dilute one's psychic and emotional perception, to the extent that one does not and cannot receive all that the other person is capable of sending.

Yet I may believe that a man whose soul or emotional apparatus had lain dormant in a deadening limbo of desuetude is capable of responding from some great sunken well of his being, as though a potent catalyst had been tossed into a critical mass, when an exciting, lovely, and lovable woman enters the range of his feelings. What a deep, slow, torturous, reluctant, frightened stirring! He feels a certain part of himself in a state of flux, as if a bodiless stranger has stolen inside his body, startling him by doing calisthenics, and he feels himself coming slowly back to life. His body chemistry changes and he is flushed with new strength.

When she first comes to him his heart is empty, a desolate place, a dehydrated oasis, unsolaced, and he's craving womanfood, without which sustenance the tension of his manhood has unwound and relaxed. He has imperative need of the kindness, sympathy, understanding, and conversation of a woman, to hear a woman's laughter at his words, to answer her questions and be answered by her, to look into her eyes, to sniff her primeval fragrance, to hear—with slaughtered ears—the sensuous rustling of frivolous garments as legs are crossed and uncrossed beneath a table, to feel the delicate, shy weight of her hand in his— how painfully and totally aware is he of her presence, her every movement! It is as if one had been left to die beneath a bush on a lonely trail. The sun is hot and the shade of the bush, if not offering an extension of life, offers at least a slowing-down of death. And just when one feels the next breath will surely be the last, a rare and rainbow-colored bird settles on a delicate twig of the bush and, with the magic of melodious trillings and beauty of plumage, charms the dying one back to life. The dying man feels the strength flowing into and through the conduits of his body from the charged atmosphere created by the presence of the bird, and he knows intuitively in his clinging to life that if the bird remains he will regain his strength and health—and live.

Seeing her image slipping away from the weak fingers of his mind as soon as she has gone, his mind fights for a token of her on which to peg memory. Jealously, he hoards the fading memory of their encounter, like a miser gloating over a folio of blue-chip stock. The unfathomable machinery of the subconscious projects an image onto the conscious mind: her bare right arm, from curve of shoulder to fingertip. (Had his lips quivered with desire to brand that soft, cool-looking flesh with a kiss of fire, had his fingers itched to caress?) Such is the magic of a woman, the female principle of nature which she embodies, and her power to resurrect and revitalize a long-isolated and lonely man.

I was twenty-two when I came to prison and of course I have changed tremendously over the years. But I had always had a strong sense of myself and in the last few years I felt I was losing my identity. There was a deadness in my body that eluded me, as though I could not exactly locate its site. I would be aware of this numbness, this feeling of atrophy, and it haunted the back of my mind. Because of this numb spot, I felt peculiarly off balance, the awareness of something missing, of a blank spot, a certain intimation of emptiness. Now I know what it was. After eight years in prison, I was visited by a woman, a woman who was interested in my work and cared about what happened to me. And since encountering her, I feel life, strength flowing back into that spot. My step, the tread of my stride, which was becoming tentative and uncertain, has begun to recover a definiteness, a confidence, a boldness which makes me want to kick over a few tables. I may even swagger a little, and, as I read in a book somewhere, "push myself forward like a train."

Four Vignettes

On Watts

Folsom Prison
August 16, 1965

As we left the Mess Hall Sunday morning and milled around in the prison yard, after four days of abortive uprising in Watts, a group of low riders [1] from Watts assembled on the basketball court. They were wearing jubilant, triumphant smiles, animated by a vicarious spirit by which they, too, were in the thick of the uprising taking place hundreds of miles away to the south in the Watts ghetto.

"Man," said one, "what they doing out there? Break it down for me, Baby."

They slapped each other's outstretched palms in a cool salute and burst out laughing with joy.

"Home boy, them Brothers is taking care of Business!" shrieked another ecstatically.

Then one low rider, stepping into the center of the circle formed by the others, rared back on his legs and swaggered,

---

[1] *Low Rider.* A Los Angeles nickname for ghetto youth. Originally the term was coined to describe the youth who had lowered the bodies of their cars so that they rode low, close to the ground; also implied was the style of driving that these youngsters perfected. Sitting behind the steering wheel and slumped low down in the seat, all that could be seen of them was from their eyes up, which used to be the cool way of driving. When these youthful hipsters alighted from their vehicles, the term *low rider* stuck with them, evolving to the point where all black ghetto youth—but *never* the soft offspring of the black bourgeoisie—are referred to as low riders.

26

hunching his belt up with his forearms as he'd seen James Cagney and George Raft do in too many gangster movies. I joined the circle. Sensing a creative moment in the offing, we all got very quiet, very still, and others passing by joined the circle and did likewise.

"Baby," he said, "They walking in fours and kicking in doors; dropping Reds [2] and busting heads; drinking wine and committing crime, shooting and looting; high-siding [3] and low-riding, setting fires and slashing tires; turning over cars and burning down bars; making Parker mad and making me glad; putting an end to that 'go slow' crap and putting sweet Watts on the map—my black ass is in Folsom this morning but my black heart is in Watts!" Tears of joy were rolling from his eyes.

It was a cleansing, revolutionary laugh we all shared, something we have not often had occasion for.

Watts was a place of shame. We used to use Watts as an epithet in much the same way as city boys used "country" as a term of derision. To deride one as a "lame," who did not know what was happening (a rustic bumpkin), the "in-crowd" of the time from L.A. would bring a cat down by saying that he had just left Watts, that he ought to go back to Watts until he had learned what was happening, or that he had just stolen enough money to move out of Watts and was already trying to play a cool part. But now, blacks are seen in Folsom saying, "I'm from Watts, Baby!"—whether true or no, but I think their meaning is clear. Confession: I, too, have participated in this game, saying, I'm from Watts. In fact, I did live there for a time, and I'm *proud* of it, the tired lamentations of Whitney Young, Roy Wilkins, and The Preacher notwithstanding.

---

[2] *Reds.* A barbiturate, called Red Devils; so called because of the color of the capsule and because they are reputed to possess a vicious kick.
[3] *High-siding.* Cutting up. Having fun at the expense of another.

Eyes

Folsom Prison,
October 28, 1965

Once I was walking down Main Street in L.A. around noon on a Saturday and it was a beautiful sunny day. I was just a young stud about sixteen, I guess, and I had one of those I-think-I'm-cute-type walks, prancing and rolling on my toes. Before me and adjacent to the sidewalk was a shoeshine stand facing in my direction. A jukebox was blaring a tune of the times and I got caught up in the music as I walked along. I was kind of walking in time to the music. Sitting up on the customer's seat was a big fine sister who was popping her fingers and wiggling to the music and smiling at me because our eyes had met. There was no one else in the shine-stand and just as I came up even with the stand the record ended and I stopped in my tracks, staring at the girl in a fascinated stupor. Then, without warning, she sang: *"Beautiful, beautiful brown eyes."*

Wow. That did me in, cleaned me out, and I realized that I was standing there gaping at her like a country fool. I was really confused and embarrassed and I cut out, completely blowing my cool. And as I split, I saw her cracking up with kicks. It really made me feel good though, and I've always treasured that memory because the incident was so penetrating.

I had quite a different experience during a factional power struggle among the Muslims in San Quentin. A right-wing brother tried to undercut me with a smear tactic:

"Brothers," he said to all of us one day, "Brother Eldridge should not be allowed to hold any position until he's been a Muslim for seven years. He's got the Mark of the Beast on him. Look at his eyes—he's got the devil's eyes."

That startled me and touched a sore spot. A lot of other brothers were also confused. But one of my friends saved the day by pointing out that "many so-called Negroes have funny beast eyes. The devils have mixed us all up. Even the Honorable Elijah Muhammad has light-colored eyes. Brother Malcolm has light-colored eyes. So don't be going around here talking like that because you're only spreading *dis*unity. The Honorable Elijah Muhammad teaches *unity*. If you call yourself a Muslim, brother, you're going to have to start thinking Positive and put down all that Negative."

The cat had to beat a hasty retreat, but I was bleeding inside.

Soul Food

Folsom Prison,
November 3, 1965

You hear a lot of jazz about Soul Food. Take chitterlings: the ghetto blacks eat them from necessity while the black bourgeoisie has turned it into a mocking slogan. Eating chitterlings is like going slumming to them. Now that they have the price of a steak, here they come prattling about Soul Food. The people in the ghetto want steaks. *Beef Steaks*. I wish I had the power to see to it that the bourgeoisie really *did* have to make it on Soul Food.

The emphasis on Soul Food is counter-revolutionary black bourgeois ideology. The main reason Elijah Muhammad outlawed pork for Negroes had nothing to do with dietary laws. The point is that when you get all those blacks cooped up in the ghetto with beef steaks on their minds—with the weight of religious fervor behind the desire to chuck—then something's got to give. The system has made allowances for the ghettoites to obtain a little pig, *but there are no provisions for the elite to give up any beef.* The walls come tumbling down.

A Religious Conversion, More or Less

Folsom Prison,
September 10, 1965

Once I was a Catholic. I was baptized, made my first Communion, my Confirmation, and I wore a Cross with Jesus on it around my neck. I prayed at night, said my Rosary, went to Confession, and said all the Hail Marys and Our Fathers to which I was sentenced by the priest. Hopelessly enamored of sin myself, yet appalled by the sins of others, I longed for Judgment Day and a trial before a jury of my peers—this was my only chance to escape the flames which I could feel already licking at my feet. I was in a California Youth Authority institution at the time, having transgressed the laws of man—God did not indict me that time; if He did, it was a secret indictment, for I was never informed of any charges brought against me. The reason I became a Catholic was that the rule of the institution held that every Sunday each inmate had to attend the church of his choice. I chose the Catholic Church because all the Negroes and Mexicans went there. The whites went to the Protestant chapel. Had I been a fool enough to go to the Protestant chapel, one black face in a sea of white, and with guerrilla warfare going on between us, I might have ended up a Christian martyr—St. Eldridge the Stupe.

It all ended one day when, at a catechism class, the priest asked if anyone present understood the mystery of the Holy Trinity. I had been studying my lessons diligently and knew by heart what I'd been taught. Up shot my hand, my heart throbbing with piety (pride) for this chance to demonstrate my knowledge of the Word. To my great shock and embarrassment, the Father announced, and it sounded like a thunderclap, that I was lying, that no one, not even the Pope, understood the Godhead, and why else did I think they called it the *mystery* of the Holy Trinity? I saw in a flash, stung to the quick by the jeers of my fellow catechumens, that I had been used, that the Father had been lying in wait for the chance to drop that thunderbolt, in order to drive home the point that the Holy Trinity was not to be taken lightly.

I had intended to explain the Trinity with an analogy to 3-in-1 oil, so it was probably just as well.

"The Christ" and His Teachings

Folsom Prison,
September 10, 1965

My first awareness of Thomas Merton came in San Quentin, back in (I believe) 1959–60. During that time, a saint walked the earth in the person of one Chris Lovdjieff. He was a teacher at San Quentin and guru to all who came to him. What did he teach? Everything. It is easier just to say he taught Lovdjieff and let it go at that. He himself claimed to be sort of a disciple of Alan W. Watts, whom he used to bring over to Q to lecture us now and then on Hinduism, Zen Buddhism, and on the ways the peoples of Asia view the universe. I never understood how "The Christ" (as I used to call Lovdjieff, to his great sorrow and pain) could sit at Watts' feet, because he always seemed to me more warm, more human, and possessed of greater wisdom than Watts displayed either in his lectures or his books. It may be that I received this impression from having been exposed more to Lovdjieff than to Watts. Yet there was something about Watts that reminded me of a slick advertisement for a labor-saving device, aimed at the American housewife, out of the center page of *Life* magazine; while Lovdjieff's central quality seemed to be pain, suffering, and a peculiar strength based on his understanding of his own helplessness, weakness, and need. Under Lovdjieff I studied world history, Oriental philosophy, Occidental philosophy, comparative religion, and economics. I could not tell one class from the other—neither could the other students and neither, I believe, could Lovdjieff. It was all Lovdjieff.

The walls of his classrooms were covered with cardboard placards which bore quotations from the world's great thinkers. There were quotes from Japanese, Eskimos, Africans, Hopi Indians, Peruvians, Voltaire, Confucius, Laotse, Jesus Christ, Moses, Mohammed, Buddha, Rabbi Hillel, Plato, Aristotle, Marx, Lenin, Mao Tse-tung, Zoroaster—and Thomas Merton, among others. Once Lovdjieff gave a lecture on Merton, reading from his works and trying to put the man's life and work in context. He seemed desperately to want us to respect Merton's vocation and choice of the contemplative life. It was an uphill battle because a prison is in many ways like a monastery. The convicts in Lovdjieff's class hated prison. We were appalled that a free man would voluntarily enter prison—or a monastery. Let me say it right out: we thought Merton was some kind of nut. We thought the same thing about Lovdjieff. My secret disgust was that in many ways I was nothing but a monk, and how I loathed that view of myself!

I was mystified by Merton and I could not believe in his

passionate defense of monkhood. I distrusted Lovdjieff on the subject of Thomas Merton. My mind heard a special pleading in his voice. In his ardent defense of Merton, Lovdjieff seemed to be defending himself, even trying to convince himself. One day Lovdjieff confided to us that he had tried to be a monk but couldn't make it. He made it, all right, without even realizing it. San Quentin was his monastery. He busied himself about the prison as though he had a special calling to minister to the prisoners. He was there day and night and on Saturdays, without fail. The officials would sometimes have to send a guard to his class to make him stop teaching, so the inmates could be locked up for the night. He was horror-stricken that they could make such a demand of him. Reluctantly, he'd sit down heavily in his seat, burdened by defeat, and tell us to go to our cells. Part of the power we gave him was that we would never leave his class unless he himself dismissed us. If a guard came and told us to leave, he got only cold stares; we would not move until Lovdjieff gave the word. He got a secret kick out of this little victory over his tormentors. If, as happened once, he was unable to make it to the prison because his car had a blowout, he'd be full of apologies and pain next day.

Lovdjieff had extracted from me my word that I would some day read Merton for myself—he did not insist upon any particular time, just "some day." Easy enough. I gave my promise. In 1963, when I was transferred from San Quentin to Folsom for being an agitator, they put me in solitary confinement. The officials did not deem it wise, at that time, to allow me to circulate among the general inmate population. I had evolved a crash program which I would immediately activate whenever I was placed in solitary: stock up on books and read, read, read; do calisthenics and forget about the rest of the world. I had learned the waste and futility of worry. (Years ago, I had stopped being one of those convicts who take a little calendar and mark off each day.) When I asked for books to read in this particular hole, a trustee brought me a list from which to make selections. On the list I was delighted to see Merton's *The Seven Storey Mountain,* his autobiography. I thought of Lovdjieff. Here was a chance to fulfill my promise.

I was tortured by that book because Merton's suffering, in his quest for God, seemed all in vain to me. At the time, I was a Black Muslim chained in the bottom of a pit by the Devil. Did I expect Allah to tear down the walls and set me free? To me, the language and symbols of religion were nothing but weapons of war. I had no other purpose for them. All the gods are dead except the god of war. I wished that Merton had stated in secular terms the reasons he withdrew from the political, economic, military, and social system into which he was born, seeking refuge in a monastery.

Despite my rejection of Merton's theistic world view, I could not keep him out of the room. He shouldered his way through the door. Welcome, Brother Merton. I give him a bear hug. Most impressive of all to me was Merton's description of New York's black ghetto—Harlem. I liked it so much I copied out the heart of it in longhand. Later, after getting out of solitary, I used to keep this passage in mind when delivering Black Muslim lectures to other prisoners. Here is an excerpt:

Here in this huge, dark, steaming slum, hundreds of thousands of Negroes are herded together like cattle, most of them with nothing to eat and nothing to do. All the senses and imagination and sensibilities and emotions and sorrows and desires and hopes and ideas of a race with vivid feelings and deep emotional reactions are forced in upon themselves, bound inward by an iron ring of frustration: the prejudice that hems them in with its four insurmountable walls. In this huge cauldron, inestimable natural gifts, wisdom, love, music, science, poetry are stamped down and left to boil with the dregs of an elementally corrupted nature, and thousands upon thousands of souls are destroyed by vice and misery and degradation, obliterated, wiped out, washed from the register of the living, dehumanized.

What has not been devoured, in your dark furnace, Harlem, by marijuana, by gin, by insanity, hysteria, syphilis?

For a while, whenever I felt myself softening, relaxing, I had only to read that passage to become once more a rigid flame of indignation. It had precisely the same effect on me that Elijah Muhammad's writings used to have, or the words of Malcolm X, or the words of any spokesman of the oppressed in any land. I vibrate sympathetically to any protest against tyranny.

But I want to tell more about Lovdjieff—The Christ.

Chris Lovdjieff had a profound mind and an ecumenical education. I got the impression that the carnage of World War II, particularly the scientific, systematic approach to genocide of the Nazi regime, had been a traumatic experience from which it was impossible for him to recover. It was as if he had seen or experienced something which had changed him forever, sickened his soul, overwhelmed him with sympathy and love for all mankind. He hated all restraints upon the human mind, the human spirit, all blind believing, all dogmatic assertion. He questioned everything.

I was never sure of just what was driving him. That he was driven there could be no doubt. There was a sense of unreality about him. It seemed that he moved about in a mist. The atmosphere he created was like the mystic spell of Khalil Gibran's poetry. He seemed always to be listening to distant music, or silent voices, or to be talking in a whisper to himself. He loved silence and said that it should only be broken for important communications, and he would expel students from his classes for distracting the others by chatting idly in the back rows. In his classes he was a dictator. He enforced certain rules which brooked no deviation—no smoking in his classroom at any time, before class, during class, at recess, or even when school was out; no talking in Lovdjieff's class unless it was pertinent to the subject at hand; no eating or chewing gum in his classroom; no profanity. Simple rules, perhaps, but in San Quentin they were visionary, adventurous, audacious. The Christ enforced them strictly. The other teachers and the guards wondered how he got away with it. We students wondered why we enthusiastically submitted to it. The Christ would look surprised, as if he did not understand, if you asked him about it. If one of the other teachers forgot and came into Lovdjieff's classroom smoking, he was sent hopping. The same went for prison guards. I can still see the shocked expression of a substitute teacher who, coming into Lovdjieff's room during recess smoking a pipe, was told: "Leave this room!"

When you came to Lovdjieff's classes, you came to learn. If you betrayed other motives, "Get out of here this minute!"—without malice but without equivocation. He was a magnet, an institution. He worked indefatigably. His day started when the school bell rang at 8 A.M. Often he would forego lunch to interview a few students and help them along with their schoolwork or personal problems. He never ceased complaining because the officials refused to allow him to eat lunch in the mess hall with the prisoners. Had they given him a cell he would have taken it. After lunch, he'd teach until 3 P.M. When night school convened at 6 P.M., The Christ would be there, beaming, radiating, and he'd teach passionately until 10 P.M. Then, reluctantly, he'd go home to suffer in exile until school opened next day. On

Saturdays he'd be there bright and early to teach—Lovdjieff. He would have come on Sundays too, only the officials put their foot down and refused to hear of it. The Christ settled for a Sunday evening radio program of two hours which he taped for broadcast to the prisoners.

His classes were works of art. He made ancient history contemporary by evoking the total environment—intellectual, social, political, economic—of an era. He breathed life into the shattered ruins of the past. Students sat entranced while The Christ performed, his silver-rimmed glasses reflecting the light in eye-twinkling flashes.

He dressed like a college boy, betraying a penchant for simple sweaters and plain slacks of no particular distinction. He burned incense in his classroom when he lectured on religion, to evoke a certain mood. He was drawn to those students who seemed most impossible to teach—old men who had been illiterate all their lives and set in their ways. Lovdjieff didn't believe that anyone or anything in the universe was "set in its ways." Those students who were intelligent and quickest to learn he seemed reluctant to bother with, almost as if to say, pointing at the illiterates and speaking to the bright ones: "Go away. Leave me. You don't need me. These others do."

Jesus wept. Lovdjieff would weep over a tragic event that had taken place ten thousand years ago in some forgotten byway in the Fertile Crescent. Once he was lecturing on the ancient Hebrews. He was angry with them for choosing to settle along the trade routes between Egypt and Mesopotamia. He showed how, over the centuries, time and time again, these people had been invaded, slaughtered, driven out, captured, but always to return.

"What is it that keeps pulling them back to this spot!" he exclaimed. He lost his breath. His face crumbled, and he broke down and wept. "Why do they insist on living in the middle of that—that [for once, I thought meanly, The Christ couldn't find a word] that—that—Freeway! They have to sit down in the center of the Freeway! That's all it is—look!" He pointed out the trade routes on the map behind his desk, then he sat down and cried uncontrollably for several minutes.

Another time, he brought tape-recorded selections from Thomas Wolfe's *Look Homeward Angel*. The Christ wept all through the tape.

The Christ could weep over a line of poetry, over a single image in a poem, over the beauty of a poem's music, over the fact that man can talk, read, write, walk, reproduce, die, eat, eliminate—over the fact that a chicken can lay an egg.

Once he lectured us all week on Love. He quoted what poets had said of Love, what novelists had said of Love, what playwrights had said of Love. He played tapes of Ashley Montagu on Love. Over the weekend, each student was to write an essay on his own conception of Love, mindful to have been influenced by what he had been listening to all week long. In my essay I explained that I did not love white people. I quoted Malcolm X:

How can I love the man who raped my mother, killed my father, enslaved my ancestors, dropped atomic bombs on Japan, killed off the Indians and keeps me cooped up in the slums? I'd rather be tied up in a sack and tossed into the Harlem River first.

Lovdjieff refused to grade my paper. He returned it to me. I protested that he was being narrow-minded and dogmatic in not understanding why I did not love white people simply because he himself was white. He told me to talk with him after class.

"How can you do this to me?" he asked.

"I've only written the way I feel," I said.

Instead of answering, he cried.

"Jesus wept," I told him and walked out.

Two days later, he returned my essay—ungraded. There were instead spots on it which I realized to be his tears.

Although Lovdjieff's popularity among the prisoners continued to soar and the waiting lists for his classes grew longer and longer, prison authorities banned his radio program. Then they stopped him from coming in on Saturdays. Then they stopped him from teaching night school. Then they took away his pass and barred him from San Quentin.

I must say that this man has not been adequately described. Certain things I hold back on purpose, others I don't know how to say. Until I began writing this, I did not know that I had a vivid memory of him. But now I can close my eyes and relive many scenes in which he goes into his act.

A Day in Folsom Prison

Folsom Prison,
September 19, 1965

My day begins officially at 7:00, when all inmates are required to get out of bed and stand before their cell doors to
be counted by guards who walk along the tier saying, "1, 2,
3 . . . " However, I never remain in bed until 7. I'm
usually up by 5:30. The first thing I do is make up my bed.
Then I pick up all my books, newspapers, etc., off the floor
of my cell and spread them over my bed to clear the floor
for calisthenics. In my cell, I have a little stool on which I
lay a large plywood board, about 2½ by 3 feet, which I use
as a typing and writing table. At night, I load this makeshift
table down with books and papers, and when I read at night
I spill things all over the floor. When I leave my cell, I set
this board, loaded down, on my bed, so that if a guard
comes into my cell to search it, he will not knock the board
off the stool, as has happened before. Still in the nude, the
way I sleep, I go through my routine: kneebends, butter-
flies, touching my toes, squats, windmills. I continue for
about half an hour.

Sometimes, if I have something I want to write or type
so that I can mail it that morning, I forgo my calisthenics.
But this is unusual. (We are required, if we want our mail
to go out on a certain day, to have it in the mailbox by
about 8:00. When we leave our cells at 7:30 to go to break-

fast, we pass right by the mailbox and drop in our mail on the way to mess hall.)

Usually, by the time I finish my calisthenics, the trustee (we call him tiertender, or keyman) comes by and fills my little bucket with hot water. We don't have hot running water ourselves. Each cell has a small sink with a cold-water tap, a bed, a locker, a shelf or two along the wall, and a commode. The trustee has a big bucket, with a long spout like the ones people use to water their flowers, only without the sprinkler. He pokes the spout through the bars and pours you about a gallon of hot water. My cell door doesn't have bars on it; it is a solid slab of steel with fifty-eight holes in it about the size of a half dollar, and a slot in the center, at eye level, about an inch wide and five inches long. The trustee sticks the spout through one of the little holes and pours my hot water, and in the evenings the guard slides my mail in to me through the slot. Through the same slot the convicts pass newspapers, books, candy, and cigarettes to one another.

When the guard has mail for me he stops at the cell door and calls my name, and I recite my number—A-29498—to verify that I am the right Cleaver. When I get mail I avert my eyes so I can't see who it's from. Then I sit down on my bed and peep at it real slowly, like a poker player peeping at his cards. I can feel when I've got a letter from you, and when I peep up on your name on the envelope I let out a big yell. It's like having four aces. But if the letter is not from you, it's like having two deuces, a three, a four, and a five, all in scrambled suits. A bum kick. Nothing. What is worse is when the guard passes my door without pausing. I can hear his keys jingling. If he stops at my door the keys sound like Christmas bells ringing, but if he keeps going they just sound like—keys.

I live in the honor block. In the other blocks, the fronts

of the cells consist of nothing but bars. When I first moved into the honor block, I didn't like it at all. The cells seemed made for a dungeon. The heavy steel doors slammed shut with a clang of finality that chilled my soul. The first time that door closed on me I had the same wild, hysterical sensation I'd felt years ago at San Quentin when they first locked me in solitary. For the briefest moment I felt like yelling out for help, and it seemed that in no circumstances would I be able to endure that cell. All in that split second I felt like calling out to the guards, pleading with them to let me out of the cell, begging them to let me go, promising them that I would be a good boy in the future.

But just as quickly as the feeling came, it went, dissolved, and I felt at peace with myself. I felt that I could endure anything, everything, even the test of being broken on the rack. I've been in every type of cell they have in the prisons of California, and the door to my present cell seems the most cruel and ugly of all. However, I have grown to like this door. When I go out of my cell, I can hardly wait to get back in, to slam that cumbersome door, and hear the sharp click as the trustee snaps the lock behind me. The trustees keep the keys to the cells of the honor block all day, relinquishing them at night, and to get into your cell, all you have to do is round up the trustee in charge of your tier. Once inside my cell, I feel safe: I don't have to watch the other convicts any more or the guards in the gun towers. If you live in a cell with nothing but bars on the front, you cannot afford to relax; someone can walk along the tier and throw a Molotov cocktail in on you before you know it, something I've seen happen in San Quentin. Whenever I live in one of those barred cells, I keep a blanket within easy reach in case of emergency, to smother a fire if need be. Paranoia? Yes, but it's the least one can do for oneself. In my present cell, with its impregnable door, I don't worry about sabotage—although if someone wanted to badly enough, they could figure something out.

Well . . . after I've finished my calisthenics and the hot water has arrived, I take me a bird (jailbird) bath in the little sink. It's usually about 6:00 by then. From then until 7:30, when we are let out for breakfast, I clean up my cell and try to catch a little news over the radio. Radio?—each cell has a pair of earphones!—with only two channels on it. The programs are monitored from the radio room. The radio schedule is made up by the radio committee, of which I am a member.

At 7:30, breakfast. From the mess hall, every day except Saturday, my day off, I go straight to the bakery, change into my white working clothes, and that's me until about noon. From noon, I am "free" until 3:20, the evening mandatory lockup, when we are required, again, to stand before our cell doors and be counted. There is another count at 6:30 P.M.—three times every day without fail.

When I'm through working in the bakery, I have the choice of (1) going to my cell; (2) staying in the dining room to watch TV; (3) going down to the library; or (4) going out to the yard to walk around, sit in the sun, lift weights, play some funny game—like checkers, chess, marbles, horseshoes, handball, baseball, shuffleboard, beating on the punching bag, basketball, talk, TV, paddle-tennis, watching the other convicts who are watching other convicts. When I first came to Folsom, I was astonished to see the old grizzled cons playing marbles. The marble players of Folsom are legendary throughout the prison system: I first heard about them years ago. There is a sense of ultimate defeat about them. Some guy might boast about how he is going to get out next time and stay out, and someone will put him down by saying he'll soon be back, playing marbles like a hasbeen, a neverwas, blasted back into childhood by a crushing defeat to his final dream. The marble players have the game down to an art, and they play all day long, fanatically absorbed in what they are doing.

If I have a cell partner who knows the game, I play him chess now and then, maybe a game each night. I have a chess set of my own and sometimes when I feel like doing nothing else, I take out a little envelope in which I keep a collection of chess problems clipped from newspapers, and run off one or two. But I have never been able to give all my time to one of these games. I am seldom able to play a game of chess out on the yard. Whenever I go out on the yard these days, I'm usually on my way to the library.

On the yard there is a little shack off to one corner which is the office of the Inmates Advisory Council (IAC). Sometimes I visit the shack to shoot the bull and get the latest drawings (news). And sometimes I go out to the weight-lifting area, strip down to a pair of trunks, and push a little iron for a while and soak up the sun.

At 3:20, lockup. Stand for count. After count, off to the evening meal. Back to the cell. Stand for count at 6:30. After the 6:30 count, we are all let out of our cells, one tier at a time, for showers, to exchange dirty socks and towels for clean ones, a haircut, then back to the cell. I duck this crush by taking my showers in the bakery. At night, I only go to exchange my linen. In the honor block, we are allowed to come out after the 6:30 count every Saturday, Sunday, and Wednesday night to watch TV until 10:00, before we are locked up for the night. The only time I went out for TV was to dig the broads on Shindig and Hollywood-A-Go-Go, but those programs don't come on anymore. We recently got the rule changed so that, on TV nights, those in the honor block can type until 10:00. It used to be that no typing was allowed after 8:00. I am very pleased to be able to get in that extra typing time: I can write you more letters.

On Thursday I go out of my cell after the 6:30 count to attend the weekly IAC meetings. These meetings adjourn promptly at 9:00. On Saturday mornings, my off day, I usually attend the meetings of the Gavel Club, but this past Saturday I was in the middle of my last letter to you and I stole away to my cell. I enjoyed it so much that I am tempted to put the Gavel Club down, but I hope that I don't because that's where I'm gaining some valuable experience and technique in public speaking.

On the average I spend approximately seventeen hours a day in my cell. I enjoy the solitude. The only drawback is that I am unable to get the type of reading material I want, and there is hardly anyone with a level head to talk to.

There are quite a few guys here who write. Seems that every convict wants to. Some of them have managed to sell a piece here and there. They have a writers' workshop which meets in the library under the wing of our librarian. I've never had a desire to belong to this workshop, partly because of my dislike for the attitude of the librarian and partly because of the phony, funny-style convicts. Mostly, I suppose, it's because the members of the workshop are all white and all sick when it comes to color. They're not all sick, but they're not for real. They're fair-weather types, not even as lukewarm as good white liberals, and they conform to the Mississippi atmosphere prevalent here in Folsom. Blacks and whites do not fraternize together in comfort here. Harry Golden's concept of vertical integration and horizontal segregation about covers it. The whites want to talk with you out on the yard or at work, standing up, but they shun you when it comes to sitting down. For instance, when we line up for chow, the lines leading into the mess halls are integrated. But once inside the mess hall, blacks sit at tables by themselves and whites sit with themselves or with the Mexicans.

There's this one Jewish stud out of New York who fell

out of Frisco. He thinks he is another Lenny Bruce. In point of fact he is funny and very glib, and I dig rapping (talking) with him. He's a hype but he is very down with the current scene. Says that he lived in North Beach and all that, and that he has this chick who writes him who is a member of the DuBois Club in Frisco. Well, this cat is well read and we exchange reading material. He says that at home he has every copy of *The Realist* published up to the time of his fall. *The Evergreen Review* kills him. We communicate pretty well and I know that stud is not a racist, but he is a conformist—which in my book is worse, more dangerous, than an out-and-out foe. The other day we were talking about the Free Speech Movement. He was reading a book by Paul Goodman, *Growing Up Absurd,* which he had with him. We were very hung up talking and then it was time for lunch. We got in line and continued our conversation. He was trying to convince me that the whole FSM was predicated on the writings of Paul Goodman, and that he had heard, with his own ears, Mario Savio say as much. Then all of a sudden I noticed this cat grow leery and start looking all around. He made me nervous. I thought maybe someone was trying to sneak up on us with a knife or something. When he kept doing this, I asked him what the fuck was the matter with him. He turned real red and said that he "just remembered" that he had to talk to another fellow. I dug right away what the kick was, so I said, "later," and he split. I'm used to such scenes, having a 400-year heritage of learning to roll with that type of punch. I saw him in the mess hall looking very pushed out of shape. I had to laugh at him. I felt that he was probably thinking that if the whites put the blacks in the gas chambers they might grab him too if he was with me. That thought tickled me a little as I watched him peeping around like a ferret. One of his points of indignation is that, he says, he will never forgive Israel for kidnaping and killing Eichmann, and he gets mad at me because I take Israel's side, just to keep the conversation alive. Too much agreement kills a chat. What really bugs him is when I say that there are many blacks who, if they were in the position, would do a little rounding up of the Eichmann types in America. A few days later he told me, "You saw through me the other day, didn't you?"

"I see through you every day," I told him. He looked as if he expected or wanted me to hit him or something. I told him that he was good for nothing but to be somebody's jailhouse wife and he laughed, then launched into a Lenny Bruce-type monologue.

My own reaction is to have as little as possible to do with the whites. I have no respect for a duck who runs up to me on the yard all buddy-buddy, and then feels obliged not to sit down with me. It's not that I'm dying to sit with him either, but there is a principle involved which cuts me deeply.

Talk about hypocrisy: you should see the library. We are allowed to order, from the state library, only non-fiction and law books. Of the law books, we can only order books containing court opinion. We can get any decision of the California District Court of Appeals, the California Supreme Court, the U.S. District Courts, the Circuit Courts, and the U.S. Supreme Court. But books of an explanatory nature are prohibited. Many convicts who do not have lawyers are forced to act *in propria persona*. They do all right. But it would be much easier if they could get books that showed them how properly to plead their cause, how to prepare their petitions and briefs. This is a perpetual sore point with the Folsom Prison Bar Association, as we call ourselves.

All of the novels one *needs* to read are unavailable, and

the librarian won't let you send for them. I asked him once if he had read a certain book.

"Oh, yes!" he exclaimed.

"What did you think of it?" I asked.

"Absolutely marvelous!" he said.

"How about letting me send to the state library for it?" I asked.

"No."

Books that one wants to read—so bad that it is a taste in the mouth, like Calvin C. Hernton's *Sex and Racism in America*—he won't let you have.

"The warden says 'no sex,' " is his perpetual squelch.

There is a book written by a New York judge which gives case histories of prostitutes. The authors explore why white prostitutes, some of them from the deepest South, had Negroes for pimps, and I wanted to reread it.

"No sex," said the librarian. He is indifferent to the fact that it is a matter of life and death to me! I don't know how he justifies this because you can go over to the inmate canteen and buy all the prurient pot-boiling anti-literature that has ever been written. But everything that "is happening" today is verboten. I've been dying to read Norman Mailer's *An American Dream,* but that too is prohibited. You can have *Reader's Digest,* but *Playboy?*—not a chance. I have long wanted to file suit in Federal Court for the right to receive *Playboy* magazine. Do you think Hugh Hefner would finance such an action? I think some very nice ideas would be liberated.

The library does have a selection of very solid material, things done from ten years ago all the way back to the Bible. But it is unsatisfactory to a stud who is trying to function in the last half of the twentieth century. Go down there and try to find Hemingway, Mailer, Camus, Sartre, Baldwin, Henry Miller, Terry Southern, Julian Mayfield,

Bellow, William Burroughs, Allen Ginsberg, Herbert Gold, Robert Gover, J. O. Killens, etc.—no action. They also have this sick thing going when it comes to books by and about Negroes. Robert F. Williams' book, *Negroes with Guns,* is not allowed any more. I ordered it from the state library before it was too popular around here. I devoured it and let a few friends read it, before the librarian dug it and put it on the blacklist. Once I ordered two books from the inmate canteen with my own money. When they arrived here from the company, the librarian impounded them, placing them on my "property" the same as they did my notebooks.

I want to devote my time to reading and writing, with everything else secondary, but I can't do that in prison. I have to keep my eyes open at all times or I won't make it. There is always some madness going on, and whether you like it or not you're involved. There is no choice in the matter: you cannot sit and wait for things to come to you. So I engage in all kinds of petty intrigue which I've found necessary to survival. It consumes a lot of time and energy. But it is necessary.

Initial Reactions on the Assassination of Malcolm X

Folsom Prison,
June 19, 1965

Sunday is Movie Day at Folsom Prison and I was sitting in the darkened hulk of Mess Hall No. 1—which convicts call "The Folsom Theatre"—watching Victor Buono in a movie called *The Strangler,* when a convict known as Silly Willie came over to where I was sitting and whispered into my ear:

"Brother J sent me in to tell you it just came over the TV that Malcolm X was shot as he addressed a rally in New York."

For a moment the earth seemed to reel in orbit. The skin all over my body tightened up. "How bad?" I asked.

"The TV didn't say," answered Silly Willie. The distress was obvious in his voice. "We was around back in Pipe Alley checking TV when a special bulletin came on. All they said was Malcolm X was shot and they were rushing him to the hospital."

"Thanks," I said to Silly Willie. I felt his reassuring hand on my shoulder as he faded away in the darkness. For a moment I pondered whether to go outside and get more information, but something made me hang back. I remember distinctly thinking that I would know soon enough. On the screen before me, Victor Buono had a woman by the throat and was frantically choking the last gasping twitches

50

of life out of her slumping body. I was thinking that if Malcolm's wounds were not too serious, that if he recovered, the shooting might prove to be a blessing in disguise: it would focus more intensified attention on him and create a windfall of sympathy and support for him throughout America's black ghettos, and so put more power into his hands. The possibility that the wounds may have been fatal, that as I sat there Malcolm was lying already dead, was excluded from my mind.

After the movie ended, as I filed outside in the long line of convicts and saw the shocked, wild expression on Brother J's face, I still could not believe that Malcolm X was dead. We mingled in the crowd of convicts milling around in the yard and were immediately surrounded by a group of Muslims, all of whom, like myself, were firm supporters of Malcolm X. He's dead, their faces said, although not one of them spoke a word. As we stood there in silence, two Negro inmates walked by and one of them said to us, "That's a goddam shame how they killed that man! Of all people, why'd they kill Malcolm? Why'n't they kill some of them Uncle-Tomming m.f.'s? I wish I could get my hands on whoever did it." And he walked away, talking and cursing to his buddy.

What does one say to his comrades at the moment when The Leader falls? All comment seems irrelevant. If the source of death is so-called natural causes, or an accident, the reaction is predictable, a feeling of impotence, humbleness, helplessness before the forces of the universe. But when the cause of death is an assassin's bullet, the overpowering desire is for vengeance. One wants to strike out, to kill, crush, destroy, to deliver a telling counterblow, to inflict upon the enemy a reciprocal, equivalent loss. But whom does one strike down at such a time if one happens to be in an anonymous, amorphous crowd of convicts in

Folsom Prison and The Leader lies dead thousands of miles away across the continent?

"I'm going to my cell," I told the tight little knot of Muslims. "Allah is the Best Knower. Everything will be made manifest in time. Give it a little time. *As-Salaam Aliakum.*"

"*Wa-Aliakum Salaam,*" the Brothers returned the salutation and we shook hands all around, the double handshake which is very popular among Muslims in California prisons. (It is so popular that one sometimes grows weary of shaking hands. If a Muslim leaves a group for a minute to go get a drink of water, he is not unlikely to shake hands all around before he leaves and again when he returns. But no one complains and the convention is respected as a gesture of unity, brotherly love, and solidarity—so meaningful in a situation where Muslims are persecuted and denied recognition and the right to function as a legitimate religion.) I headed for my cell. I lived in No. 5 Building, which is Folsom's Honor Unit, reserved for those who have maintained a clean record for at least six months. Advantages: a larger cell, TV every Wednesday, Saturday, and Sunday night, less custodial supervision, easier ingress and egress. If while living in the Honor Unit you get into a "beef" which results in action against you by the disciplinary committee, one of the certain penalties is that you are immediately kicked out of No. 5 Building.

As I walked along the first tier toward my cell, I ran into Red, who lived near me on the tier.

"I guess you heard about Malcolm?"

"Yeah," I said. "They say he got wasted."

Red, who is white, knew from our many discussions that I was extremely partial to Malcolm, and he himself, being thoroughly alienated from the *status quo,* recognized the assassination for what it was: a negative blow against a positive force. Red's questions were the obvious ones: Who? Why? The questions were advanced tentatively, cautiously, because of the treacherous ground he was on: a red-headed, blue-eyed white man concerned by an event which so many others greeted with smiles and sighs. I went into my cell.

Although I heard it blared over the radio constantly and read about it in all the newspapers, days passed during which my mind continued to reject the fact of Malcolm's death. I existed in a dazed state, wandering in a trance around Folsom, drifting through the working hours in the prison bakery; and yet I was keen to observe the effect of the assassination on my fellow inmates. From most of the whites there was a leer and a hint of a smile in the eyes. They seemed anxious to see a war break out between the followers of Elijah and the followers of Malcolm.

There are only a few whites in Folsom with whom I would ever discuss the death of Malcolm or anything else besides baseball or the weather. Many of the Mexican-Americans were sympathetic, although some of them made a point, when being observed by whites, of letting drop sly remarks indicating they were glad Malcolm was gone. Among the Negroes there was mass mourning for Malcolm X. Nobody talked much for a few days. The only Negroes who were not indignant were a few of the Muslims who remained loyal to Elijah Muhammad. They interpreted Malcolm's assassination as the will of Allah descending upon his head for having gone astray. To them, it was Divine chastisement and a warning to those whom Malcolm had tempted. It was not so much Malcolm's death that made them glad; but in their eyes it now seemed possible to heal the schism in the movement and restore the monolithic unity of the Nation of Islam, a unity they looked back on with some nostalgia.

Many Negro convicts saw Malcolm's assassination as a historic turning point in black America. Whereas Negroes often talk heatedly about wiping out all the so-called Negro leaders whom they do not happen to like or agree with, this was the first significant case of Negro leader-killing that anyone could remember. What struck me is that the Negro convicts welcomed the new era. If a man as valuable to us as Malcolm could go down, then as far as I was concerned so could any other man—myself included. Coming a week after the alleged exposé of the alleged plot to dynamite the Statue of Liberty, Washington Monument, and the Liberty Bell, a plot supposedly hatched by discontented blacks, the assassination of Malcolm X had put new ideas in the wind with implications for the future of black struggle in America.

I suppose that like many of the brothers and sisters in the Nation of Islam movement, I also had clung to the hope that, somehow, the rift between Malcolm X and Elijah Muhammad would be mended. As long as Brother Malcolm was alive, many Muslims could maintain this hope, neatly overlooking the increasing bitterness of their rivalry. But death made the split final and sealed it for history. These events caused a profound personal crisis in my life and beliefs, as it did for other Muslims. During the bitter time of his suspension and prior to his break with Elijah Muhammad, we had watched Malcolm X as he sought frantically to reorient himself and establish a new platform. It was like watching a master do a dance with death on a highstrung tightrope. He pirouetted, twirled, turned somersaults in the air—but he landed firmly on his feet and was off and running. We watched it all, seeking a cause to condemn Malcolm X and cast him out of our hearts. We read all the charges and countercharges. I found Malcolm X blameless.

It had been my experience that the quickest way to become hated by the Muslims was to criticize Elijah Muhammad or disagree with something he wrote or said. If Elijah wrote, as he has done, that the swine is a poison creature composed of ⅓ rat, ⅓ cat, and ⅓ dog and you attempted to cite scientific facts to challenge this, you had sinned against the light, that was all there was to it. How much more unlikely was it, therefore, that Muslims would stand up and denounce Elijah himself, repudiate his authority and his theology, deny his revelation, and take sides against him, the Messenger of Almighty God Allah? I never dreamed that someday I would be cast in that hapless role.

After Malcolm made his pilgrimage to Mecca, completing a triumphal tour of Africa and the Near East, during which he received the high honors of a visiting dignitary, he returned to the U.S.A. and set about building his newly founded Organization of Afro-American Unity. He also established the Muslim Mosque, Inc., to receive the Muslims he thought would pull away from Elijah. The Muslim Mosque would teach Orthodox Islam, under the direction of Sheikh Ahmed Hassoun from the Holy City of Mecca. Grand Sheik Muhammad Sarur Al-Sabban, secretary-general of the Muslim World League, had offered the services of Sheikh Ahmed, according to the Los Angeles *Herald-Dispatch,* to "help Malcolm X in his efforts to correct the distorted image that the religion of Islam has been given by hate groups in this country."

I began defending Malcolm X. At a secret meeting of the Muslims in Folsom, I announced that I was no longer a follower of Elijah Muhammad, that I was throwing my support behind Brother Malcolm. I urged everyone there to think the matter over and make a choice, because it was no longer possible to ride two horses at the same time. On the wall of my cell I had a large, framed picture of Elijah Muhammad which I had had for years. I took it down, destroyed it, and in its place put up, in the same frame, a beautiful picture of Malcolm X kneeling down in the Mohammed Ali Mosque in Cairo, which I clipped from the *Saturday Evening Post*. At first the other Muslims in Folsom denounced me; some I'd known intimately for years stopped speaking to me or even looking at me. When we met, they averted their eyes. To them the choice was simple: Elijah Muhammad is the hand-picked Messenger of Allah, the instrument of Allah's Will. All who oppose him are aiding Allah's enemies, the White Devils. Whom do you choose, God or the Devil? Malcolm X, in the eyes of Elijah's followers, had committed the unforgivable heresy when, changing his views and abandoning the racist position, he admitted the possibility of brotherhood between blacks and whites. In a letter sent back to the U.S. from the Holy Land, Malcolm X had stated:

You may be shocked by these words coming from me, but I have always been a man who tries to face facts and to accept the reality of life as new experiences and knowledge unfold it. The experiences of this pilgrimage have taught me much and each hour in the Holy Land opens my eyes even more. . . . I have eaten from the same plate with people whose eyes were the bluest of blue, whose hair was the blondest of blond and whose skin was the whitest of white . . . and I felt the sincerity in the words and deeds of these "white" Muslims that I felt among the African Muslims of Nigeria, Sudan and Ghana.

Many of us were shocked and outraged by these words from Malcolm X, who had been a major influence upon us all and the main factor in many of our conversions to the Black Muslims. But there were those of us who were glad to be liberated from a doctrine of hate and racial supremacy.

The onus of teaching racial supremacy and hate, which is the white man's burden, is pretty hard to bear. Asked if he would accept whites as members of his Organization of Afro-American Unity, Malcolm said he would accept John Brown if he were around today—which certainly is setting the standard high.

At the moment I declared myself for Malcolm X, I had some prestige among the Muslims in the prisons of California, because of my active role in proselytizing new converts and campaigning for religious freedom for Muslim convicts. We sent a barrage of letters and petitions to the courts, governmental officials, even the United Nations.

After the death of Brother Booker T. X, who was shot dead by a San Quentin prison guard, and who at the time had been my cell partner and the inmate Minister of the Muslims of San Quentin, my leadership of the Muslims of San Quentin had been publicly endorsed by Elijah Muhammad's west coast representative, Minister John Shabazz of Muhammad's Los Angeles Mosque. This was done because of the explosive conditions in San Quentin at the time. Muslim officials wanted to avert any Muslim-initiated violence, which had become a distinct possibility in the aftermath of Brother Booker's death. I was instructed to impose an iron discipline upon the San Quentin Mosque, which had continued to exist despite the unending efforts of prison authorities to stamp it out. Most of the Muslims who were in prison during those days have since been released. I was one of the few remaining, and I was therefore looked upon by the other Muslims as one who had sacrificed and invested much in the struggle to advance the teachings of Elijah Muhammad. For that reason, my defection to Malcolm X caused a great deal of consternation among the Muslims of Folsom. But slowly, Malcolm was getting his machine together and it was obvious to me that his influence was growing. Negro inmates who had had reservations about Malcolm while he was under Elijah's authority now embraced him, and it was clear that they accepted Malcolm's leadership. Negroes whom we had tried in vain for years to convert to Elijah's fold now lined up with enthusiasm behind Malcolm.

I ran a regular public relations campaign for Malcolm in Folsom. I saw to it that copies of his speeches were made and circulated among Negro inmates. I never missed a chance to speak favorably about Malcolm, to quote him, to explain and justify what he was trying to do. Soon I had the ear of the Muslims, and it was not long before Malcolm had other ardent defenders in Folsom. In a very short time Malcolm became the hero of the vast majority of Negro inmates. Elijah Muhammad was quickly becoming irrelevant, passé.

Malcolm X had a special meaning for black convicts. A former prisoner himself, he had risen from the lowest depths to great heights. For this reason he was a symbol of hope, a model for thousands of black convicts who found themselves trapped in the vicious PPP cycle: prison-parole-prison. One thing that the judges, policemen, and administrators of prisons seem never to have understood, and for which they certainly do not make any allowances, is that Negro convicts, basically, rather than see themselves as criminals and perpetrators of misdeeds, look upon themselves as prisoners of war, the victims of a vicious, dog-eat-dog social system that is so heinous as to cancel out their own malefactions: in the jungle there is no right or wrong.

Rather than owing and paying a debt to society, Negro prisoners feel that they are being abused, that their imprisonment is simply another form of the oppression which they have known all their lives. Negro inmates feel that they are being robbed, that it is "society" that owes them, that should be paying them, a debt.

America's penology does not take this into account. Malcolm X did, and black convicts know that the ascension to power of Malcolm X or a man like him would eventually have revolutionized penology in America. Malcolm delivered a merciless and damning indictment of prevailing penology. It is only a matter of time until the question of the prisoner's debt to society versus society's debt to the prisoner is injected forcefully into national and state politics, into the civil and human rights struggle, and into the consciousness of the body politic. It is an explosive issue which goes to the very root of America's system of justice, the structure of criminal law, the prevailing beliefs and attitudes toward the convicted felon. While it is easier to make out a case for black convicts, the same principles apply to white and Mexican-American convicts as well. They too are victimized, albeit a little more subtly, by "society." When black convicts start demanding a new dispensation and definition of justice, naturally the white and Mexican-American convicts will demand equality of treatment. Malcolm X was a focus for these aspirations.

The Black Muslim movement was destroyed the moment Elijah cracked the whip over Malcolm's head, because it was not the Black Muslim movement itself that was so irresistibly appealing to the true believers. It was the awakening into self-consciousness of twenty million Negroes which was so compelling. Malcolm X articulated their aspirations better than any other man of our time. When he spoke under the banner of Elijah Muhammad he was irresistible. When he spoke under his own banner he was still irresistible. If he had become a Quaker, a Catholic, or a Seventh-Day Adventist, or a Sammy Davis-style Jew, and if he had continued to give voice to the mute ambitions in the black man's soul, his message would still have been triumphant: because what was great was not Malcolm X but the truth he uttered.

The truth which Malcolm uttered had vanquished the whole passle of so-called Negro leaders and spokesmen who trifle and compromise with the truth in order to curry favor with the white power structure. He was stopped in the only way such a man can be stopped, in the same way that the enemies of the Congolese people had to stop Lumumba, by the same method that exploiters, tyrants, and parasitical oppressors have always crushed the legitimate strivings of people for freedom, justice, and equality—by murder, assassination, and mad-dog butchery.

What provoked the assassins to murder? Did it bother them that Malcolm was elevating our struggle into the international arena through his campaign to carry it before the United Nations? Well, by murdering him they only hastened the process, because we certainly are going to take our cause before a sympathetic world. Did it bother the assassins that Malcolm denounced the racist strait-jacket demonology of Elijah Muhammad? Well, we certainly do denounce it and will continue to do so. Did it bother the assassins that Malcolm taught us to defend ourselves? We shall not remain a defenseless prey to the murderer, to the sniper and the bomber. Insofar as Malcolm spoke the truth, the truth will triumph and prevail and his name shall live; and insofar as those who opposed him lied, to that extent will their names become curses. Because "truth crushed to earth shall rise again."

So now Malcolm is no more. The bootlickers, Uncle Toms, lackeys, and stooges of the white power structure have done their best to denigrate Malcolm, to root him out of his people's heart, to tarnish his memory. But their million-worded lies fall on deaf ears. As Ossie Davis so eloquently expressed it in his immortal eulogy of Malcolm:

If you knew him you would know why we must honor him: Malcolm was our manhood, our living, black manhood! This was his meaning to his people. And, in honoring him, we honor the best in ourselves. . . . However much we may have differed with him—or with each other about him and his value as a man, let his going from us serve only to bring us together, now. Consigning these mortal remains to earth, the common mother of all, secure in the knowledge that what we place in the ground is no more now a man—but a seed—which, after the winter of our discontent will come forth again to meet us. And we will know him then for what he was and is—a Prince—our own black shining Prince!—who didn't hesitate to die, because he loved us so.

We shall have our manhood. We shall have it or the earth will be leveled by our attempts to gain it.

II: Blood of the Beast

The White Race
and Its Heroes

White people cannot, in the generality, be taken as models of how to live. Rather, the white man is himself in sore need of new standards, which will release him from his confusion and place him once again in fruitful communion with the depths of his own being.

James Baldwin
—*The Fire Next Time*

Right from the go, let me make one thing absolutely clear: I am not now, nor have I ever been, a white man. Nor, I hasten to add, am I now a Black Muslim—although I used to be. But I *am* an Ofay Watcher, a member of that unchartered, amorphous league which has members on all continents and the islands of the seas. Ofay Watchers Anonymous, we might be called, because we exist concealed in the shadows wherever colored people have known oppression by whites, by white enslavers, colonizers, imperialists, and neo-colonialists.

Did it irritate you, compatriot, for me to string those epithets out like that? Tolerate me. My intention was not necessarily to sprinkle salt over anyone's wounds. I did it primarily to relieve a certain pressure on my brain. Do you cop that? If not, then we're in trouble, because we Ofay Watchers have a pronounced tendency to slip into that mood. If it is bothersome to you, it is quite a task for me because not too long ago it was my way of life to preach, as ardently as I could, that the white race is a race of devils, created by their maker to do evil, and make evil appear as good; that the white race is the natural, unchangeable enemy of the black man, who is the original man, owner, maker, cream of the planet Earth; that the white race was soon to be destroyed by Allah, and that the black man would then inherit the earth, which has always, in fact, been his.

I have, so to speak, washed my hands in the blood of the martyr, Malcolm X, whose retreat from the precipice of madness created new room for others to turn about in, and I am now caught up in that tiny space, attempting a maneuver of my own. Having renounced the teachings of Elijah Muhammad, I find that a rebirth does not follow automatically, of its own accord, that a void is left in one's vision, and this void seeks constantly to obliterate itself by pulling one back to one's former outlook. I have tried a tentative compromise by adopting a select vocabulary, so that now when I see the whites of *their* eyes, instead of saying "devil" or "beast" I say "imperialist" or "colonialist," and everyone seems to be happier.

In silence, we have spent our years watching the ofays, trying to understand them, on the principle that you have a better chance coping with the known than with the unknown. Some of us have been, and some still are, interested in learning whether it is *ultimately* possible to live in the same territory with people who seem so disagreeable to live with; still others want to get as far away from ofays as possible. What we share in common is the desire to break the ofays' power over us.

At times of fundamental social change, such as the era in which we live, it is easy to be deceived by the onrush of events, beguiled by the craving for social stability into mistaking transitory phenomena for enduring reality. The strength and permanence of "white backlash" in America is just such an illusion. However much this rear-guard action might seem to grow in strength, the initiative, and the future, rest with those whites and blacks who have liberated themselves from the master/slave syndrome. And these are to be found mainly among the youth.

Over the past twelve years there has surfaced a political conflict between the generations that is deeper, even, than the struggle between the races. Its first dramatic manifestation was within the ranks of the Negro people, when college students in the South, fed up with Uncle Tom's hat-in-hand approach to revolution, threw off the yoke of the NAACP. When these students initiated the first sit-ins, their spirit spread like a raging fire across the nation, and the technique of non-violent direct action, constantly refined and honed into a sharp cutting tool, swiftly matured. The older Negro "leaders," who are now all die-hard advocates of this tactic, scolded the students for sitting-in. The students rained down contempt upon their hoary heads. In the pre-sit-in days, these conservative leaders had always succeeded in putting down insurgent elements among the Negro people. (A measure of their power, prior to the students' rebellion, is shown by their success in isolating such great black men as the late W. E. B. DuBois and Paul Robeson, when these stalwarts, refusing to bite their tongues, lost favor with the U.S. government by their unstinting efforts to link up the Negro revolution with national liberation movements around the world.)

The "Negro leaders," and the whites who depended upon them to control their people, were outraged by the impudence of the students. Calling for a moratorium on student initiative, they were greeted instead by an encore of sit-ins, and retired to their ivory towers to contemplate the new phenomenon. Others, less prudent because held on a tighter leash by the whites, had their careers brought to an abrupt end because they thought they could lead a black/white backlash against the students, only to find themselves in a kind of Bay of Pigs. Negro college presidents, who expelled students from all-Negro colleges in an attempt to quash the demonstrations, ended up losing their jobs; the victorious students would no longer allow them to preside over the campuses. The spontaneous protests on southern campuses over the repressive measures of their college administrations were an earnest of the Free Speech upheaval which years later was to shake the UC campus at Berkeley. In countless ways, the rebellion of the black students served as catalyst for the brewing revolt of the whites.

What has suddenly happened is that the white race has lost its heroes. Worse, its heroes have been revealed as villains and its greatest heroes as the arch-villains. The new generations of whites, appalled by the sanguine and despicable record carved over the face of the globe by their race in the last five hundred years, are rejecting the panoply of white heroes, whose heroism consisted in erecting the inglorious edifice of colonialism and imperialism; heroes whose careers rested on a system of foreign and domestic exploitation, rooted in the myth of white supremacy and the manifest destiny of the white race. The emerging shape of a new world order, and the requisites for survival in such a world, are fostering in young whites a new outlook. They recoil in shame from the spectacle of cowboys and pioneers—their heroic forefathers whose exploits filled earlier generations with pride—galloping across a movie screen shooting down Indians like Coke bottles. Even Winston Churchill, who is looked upon by older whites as perhaps the greatest hero of the twentieth century—even he, because of the system of which he was a creature and which he served, is an arch-villain in the eyes of the young white rebels.

At the close of World War Two, national liberation movements in the colonized world picked up new momentum and audacity, seeking to cash in on the democratic promises made by the Allies during the war. The Atlantic Charter, signed by President Roosevelt and Prime Minister Churchill in 1941, affirming "the right of all people to choose the form of government under which they may live," established the principle, although it took years of postwar struggle to give this piece of rhetoric even the appearance of reality. And just as world revolution has prompted the oppressed to re-evaluate their self-image in terms of the changing conditions, to slough off the servile attitudes inculcated by long years of subordination, the same dynamics of change have prompted the white people of the world to re-evaluate their self-image as well, to disabuse themselves of the Master Race psychology developed over centuries of imperial hegemony.

It is among the white youth of the world that the greatest change is taking place. It is they who are experiencing the great psychic pain of waking into consciousness to find their inherited heroes turned by events into villains. Communication and understanding between the older and younger generations of whites has entered a crisis. The elders, who, in the tradition of privileged classes or races, genuinely do not understand the youth, trapped by old ways of thinking and blind to the future, have only just begun to be vexed —because the youth have only just begun to rebel. So thoroughgoing is the revolution in the psyches of white youth that the traditional tolerance which every older generation has found it necessary to display is quickly exhausted, leaving a gulf of fear, hostility, mutual mis-understanding, and contempt.

The rebellion of the oppressed peoples of the world, along with the Negro revolution in America, have opened the way to a new evaluation of history, a re-examination of the role played by the white race since the beginning of European expansion. The positive achievements are also there in the record, and future generations will applaud them. But there can be no applause now, not while the master still holds the whip in his hand! Not even the master's own children can find it possible to applaud him —he cannot even applaud himself! The negative rings too loudly. Slave-catchers, slaveowners, murderers, butchers, invaders, oppressors—the white heroes have acquired new names. The great white statesmen whom school children are taught to revere are revealed as the architects of systems of human exploitation and slavery. Religious leaders are exposed as condoners and justifiers of all these evil deeds. Schoolteachers and college professors are seen as a clique of brainwashers and whitewashers.

The white youth of today are coming to see, intuitively, that to escape the onus of the history their fathers made they must face and admit the moral truth concerning the works of their fathers. That such venerated figures as George Washington and Thomas Jefferson owned hundreds of black slaves, that all of the Presidents up to Lincoln presided over a slave state, and that every President since Lincoln connived politically and cynically with the issues affecting the human rights and general welfare of the broad masses of the American people—these facts weigh heavily upon the hearts of these young people.

The elders do not like to give these youngsters credit for being able to understand what is going on and what has gone on. When speaking of juvenile delinquency, or the rebellious attitude of today's youth, the elders employ a glib rhetoric. They speak of the "alienation of youth," the desire of the young to be independent, the problems of "the father image" and "the mother image" and their effect upon growing children who lack sound models upon which to pattern themselves. But they consider it bad form to connect the problems of the youth with the central event of our era— the national liberation movements abroad and the Negro revolution at home. The foundations of authority have been blasted to bits in America because the whole society has been indicted, tried, and convicted of injustice. To the youth, the elders are Ugly Americans; to the elders, the youth have gone mad.

The rebellion of the white youth has gone through four broadly discernible stages. First there was an initial recoiling away, a rejection of the conformity which America expected, and had always received, sooner or later, from its youth. The disaffected youth were refusing to participate in the system, having discovered that America, far from helping the underdog, was up to its ears in the mud trying to hold the dog down. Because of the publicity and self-advertisements of the more vocal rebels, this period has come to be known as the beatnik era, although not all of the youth affected by these changes thought of themselves as beatniks. The howl of the beatniks and their scathing, outraged denunciation of the system—characterized by Ginsberg as Moloch, a bloodthirsty Semitic deity to which the ancient tribes sacrificed their firstborn children—was a serious, irrevocable declaration of war. It is revealing that the elders looked upon the beatniks as mere obscene misfits who were too lazy to take baths and too stingy to buy a haircut. The elders had eyes but couldn't see, ears but couldn't hear—not even when the message came through as clearly as in this remarkable passage from Jack Kerouac's *On the Road:*

At lilac evening I walked with every muscle aching among the lights of 27th and Welton in the Denver colored section, wishing I were a Negro, feeling that the best the white world had offered was not enough ecstasy for me, not enough life, joy, kicks, darkness, music, not enough night. I wished I were a Denver Mexican, or even a poor overworked Jap, anything but what I so drearily was, a "white man" disillusioned. All my life I'd had white ambitions. . . . I passed the dark porches of Mexican and Negro homes; soft voices were there, occasionally the dusky knee of some mysterious sensuous gal; the dark faces of the men behind rose arbors. Little children sat like sages in ancient rocking chairs.

The second stage arrived when these young people, having decided emphatically that the world, and particularly the U.S.A., was unacceptable to them in its present form, began an active search for roles they could play in changing the society. If many of these young people were content to lay up in their cool beat pads, smoking pot and listening to jazz in a perpetual orgy of esoteric bliss, there were others, less crushed by the system, who recognized the need for positive action. Moloch could not ask for anything more than to have its disaffected victims withdraw into safe, passive, apolitical little nonparticipatory islands, in an economy less and less able to provide jobs for the growing pool of unemployed. If all the unemployed had followed the lead of the beatniks, Moloch would gladly have legalized the use of euphoric drugs and marijuana, passed out free jazz albums and sleeping bags, to all those willing to sign affidavits promising to remain "beat." The non-beat disenchanted white youth were attracted magnetically to the Negro revo-lution, which had begun to take on a mass, insurrectionary tone. But they had difficulty understanding their relat ship to the Negro, and what role "whites" could play in "Negro revolution." For the time being they watched the Negro activists from afar.

The third stage, which is rapidly drawing to a close, emerged when white youth started joining Negro demonstrations in large numbers. The presence of whites among the demonstrators emboldened the Negro leaders and allowed them to use tactics they never would have been able to employ with all-black troops. The racist conscience of America is such that murder does not register as murder, really, unless the victim is white. And it was only when the newspapers and magazines started carrying pictures and stories of white demonstrators being beaten and maimed by mobs and police that the public began to protest. Negroes have become so used to this double standard that they, too, react differently to the death of a white. When white freedom riders were brutalized along with blacks, a sigh of relief went up from the black masses, because the blacks knew that white blood is the coin of freedom in a land where for four hundred years black blood has been shed unremarked and with impunity. America has never truly been outraged by the murder of a black man, woman, or child. White politicians may, if Negroes are aroused by a particular murder, say with their lips what they know with their minds they should feel with their hearts—but don't.

It is a measure of what the Negro feels that when the two white and one black civil rights workers were murdered in Mississippi in 1964, the event was welcomed by Negroes on a level of understanding beyond and deeper than the grief they felt for the victims and their families. This welcoming of violence and death to whites can almost be heard—indeed it can be heard—in the inevitable words, oft repeated by Negroes, that those whites, and blacks, do not die

in vain. So it was with Mrs. Viola Liuzzo. And much of the
anger which Negroes felt toward Martin Luther King during the Battle of Selma stemmed from the fact that he
denied history a great moment, never to be recaptured,
when he turned tail on the Edmund Pettus Bridge and
refused to all those whites behind him what they had
traveled thousands of miles to receive. If the police had
turned them back by force, all those nuns, priests, rabbis,
preachers, and distinguished ladies and gentlemen old and
young—as they had done the Negroes a week earlier—the
violence and brutality of the system would have been ruth-
lessly exposed. Or if, seeing King determined to lead them
on to Montgomery, the troopers had stepped aside to avoid
precisely the confrontation that Washington would not have
tolerated, it would have signaled the capitulation of the
militant white South. As it turned out, the March on Montgomery was a show of somewhat dim luster, stage-managed
by the Establishment. But by this time the young whites
were already active participants in the Negro revolution. In
fact they had begun to transform it into something broader,
with the potential of encompassing the whole of America in
a radical reordering of society.

The fourth stage, now in its infancy, sees these white
youth taking the initiative, using techniques learned in the
Negro struggle to attack problems in the general society.
The classic example of this new energy in action was the
student battle on the UC campus at Berkeley, California—
the Free Speech Movement. Leading the revolt were vet-
erans of the civil rights movement, some of whom spent
time on the firing line in the wilderness of Mississippi/Ala-
bama. Flowing from the same momentum were student
demonstrations against U.S. interference in the internal
affairs of Vietnam, Cuba, the Dominican Republic, and the
Congo and U.S. aid to apartheid in South Africa. The stu-

dents even aroused the intellectual community to actions and positions unthinkable a few years ago: witness the teach-ins. But their revolt is deeper than single-issue protest. The characteristics of the white rebels which most alarm their elders—the long hair, the new dances, their love for Negro music, their use of marijuana, their mystical attitude toward sex—are all tools of their rebellion. They have turned these tools against the totalitarian fabric of American society—and they mean to change it.

From the beginning, America has been a schizophrenic nation. Its two conflicting images of itself were never reconciled, because never before has the survival of its most cherished myths made a reconciliation mandatory. Once before, during the bitter struggle between North and South climaxed by the Civil War, the two images of America came into conflict, although whites North and South scarcely understood it. The image of America held by its most alienated citizens was advanced neither by the North nor by the South; it was perhaps best expressed by Frederick Douglass, who was born into slavery in 1817, escaped to the North, and became the greatest leader-spokesman for the blacks of his era. In words that can still, years later, arouse an audience of black Americans, Frederick Douglass delivered, in 1852, a scorching indictment in his Fourth of July oration in Rochester:

What to the American slave is your Fourth of July? I answer: a day that reveals to him, more than all other days in the year, the gross injustice and cruelty to which he is the constant victim. To him your celebration is a sham; your boasted liberty, an unholy licence; your national greatness, swelling vanity; your sounds of rejoicing are empty and heartless; your denunciation of tyrants, brass-fronted impudence; your shouts of liberty and equality, hollow mockery; your prayers and hymns, your sermons and thanksgivings, with all your religious parade and solemnity, are,

to him, more bombast, fraud, deception, impiety and hypocrisy
—a thin veil to cover up crimes which would disgrace a nation
of savages. . . .

You boast of your love of liberty, your superior civilization,
and your pure Christianity, while the whole political power of
the nation (as embodied in the two great political parties) is
solemnly pledged to support and perpetuate the enslavement of
three millions of your countrymen. You hurl your anathemas at
the crown-headed tyrants of Russia and Austria and pride yourselves on your democratic institutions, while you yourselves
consent to be the mere *tools* and *bodyguards* of the tyrants of
Virginia and Carolina.

You invite to your shores fugitives of oppression from
abroad, honor them with banquets, greet them with ovations,
cheer them, toast them, salute them, protect them, and pour out
your money to them like water; but the fugitive from your own
land you advertise, hunt, arrest, shoot, and kill. You glory in
your refinement and your universal education; yet you maintain
a system as barbarous and dreadful as ever stained the character of a nation—a system begun in avarice, supported in
pride, and perpetuated in cruelty.

You shed tears over fallen Hungary, and make the sad story
of her wrongs the theme of your poets, statesmen and orators,
till your gallant sons are ready to fly to arms to vindicate her
cause against the oppressor; but, in regard to the ten thousand
wrongs of the American slave, you would enforce the strictest
silence, and would hail him as an enemy of the nation who
dares to make these wrongs the subject of public discourse!

This most alienated view of America was preached by
the Abolitionists, and by Harriet Beecher Stowe in her
Uncle Tom's Cabin. But such a view of America was too
distasteful to receive wide attention, and serious debate
about America's image and her reality was engaged in only
on the fringes of society. Even when confronted with over-

whelming evidence to the contrary, most white Americans have found it possible, after steadying their rattled nerves, to settle comfortably back into their vaunted belief that America is dedicated to the proposition that all men are created equal and endowed by their Creator with certain inalienable rights—life, liberty and the pursuit of happiness. With the Constitution for a rudder and the Declaration of Independence as its guiding star, the ship of state is sailing always toward a brighter vision of freedom and justice for all.

Because there is no common ground between these two contradictory images of America, they had to be kept apart. But the moment the blacks were let into the white world— let out of the voiceless and faceless cages of their ghettos, singing, walking, talking, dancing, writing, and orating *their* image of America and of Americans—the white world was suddenly challenged to match its practice to its preachments. And this is why those whites who abandon the *white* image of America and adopt the *black* are greeted with such unmitigated hostility by their elders.

For all these years whites have been taught to believe in the myth they preached, while Negroes have had to face the bitter reality of what America practiced. But without the lies and distortions, white Americans would not have been able to do the things they have done. When whites are forced to look honestly upon the objective proof of their deeds, the cement of mendacity holding white society together swiftly disintegrates. On the other hand, the core of the black world's vision remains intact, and in fact begins to expand and spread into the psychological territory vacated by the non-viable white lies, i.e., into the minds of young whites. It is remarkable how the system worked for so many years, how the majority of whites remained effectively unaware of any contradiction between their view of the world and that world itself. The mechanism by which this was rendered possible requires examination at this point.

Let us recall that the white man, in order to justify slavery and, later on, to justify segregation, elaborated a complex, all-pervasive myth which at one time classified the black man as a subhuman beast of burden. The myth was progressively modified, gradually elevating the blacks on the scale of evolution, following their slowly changing status, until the plateau of separate-but-equal was reached at the close of the nineteenth century. During slavery, the black was seen as a mindless Supermasculine Menial. Forced to do the backbreaking work, he was conceived in terms of his ability to do such work—"field niggers," etc. The white man administered the plantation, doing all the thinking, exercising omnipotent power over the slaves. He had little difficulty dissociating himself from the black slaves, and he could not conceive of their positions being reversed or even reversible.

Blacks and whites being conceived as mutually exclusive types, those attributes imputed to the blacks could not also be imputed to the whites—at least not in equal degree—without blurring the line separating the races. These images were based upon the social function of the two races, the work they performed. The ideal white man was one who knew how to use his head, who knew how to manage and control things and get things done. Those whites who were not in a position to perform these functions nevertheless aspired to them. The ideal black man was one who did exactly as he was told, and did it efficiently and cheerfully. "Slaves," said Frederick Douglass, "are generally expected to sing as well as to work." As the black man's position and function became more varied, the images of white and black, having become stereotypes, lagged behind.

The separate-but-equal doctrine was promulgated by the

Supreme Court in 1896. It had the same purpose domestically as the Open Door Policy toward China in the international arena: to stabilize a situation and subordinate a non-white population so that racist exploiters could manipulate those people according to their own selfish interests. These doctrines were foisted off as *the epitome of enlightened justice, the highest expression of morality.* Sanctified by religion, justified by philosophy and legalized by the Supreme Court, separate-but-equal was enforced by day by agencies of the law, and by the KKK & Co. under cover of night. Booker T. Washington, the Martin Luther King of his day, accepted separate-but-equal in the name of all Negroes. W. E. B. DuBois denounced it.

Separate-but-equal marked the last stage of the white man's flight into cultural neurosis, and the beginning of the black man's frantic striving to assert his humanity and equalize his position with the white. Blacks ventured into all fields of endeavor to which they could gain entrance. Their goal was to present in all fields a performance that would equal or surpass that of the whites. It was long axiomatic among blacks that a black had to be twice as competent as a white in any field in order to win grudging recognition from the whites. This produced a pathological motivation in the blacks to equal or surpass the whites, and a pathological motivation in the whites to maintain a distance from the blacks. This is the rack on which black and white Americans receive their delicious torture! At first there was the color bar, flatly denying the blacks entrance to certain spheres of activity. When this no longer worked, and blacks invaded sector after sector of American life and economy, the whites evolved other methods of keeping their distance. The illusion of the Negro's inferior nature had to be maintained.

One device evolved by the whites was to tab whatever the

blacks did with the prefix "Negro." We had *Negro* literature, *Negro* athletes, *Negro* music, *Negro* doctors, *Negro*
politicians, *Negro* workers. The malignant ingeniousness of
this device is that although it accurately describes an objective biological fact—or, at least, a sociological fact in
America—it concealed the paramount psychological fact:
that to the white mind, prefixing anything with "Negro"
automatically consigned it to an inferior category. A well-
known example of the white necessity to deny due credit to
blacks is in the realm of music. White musicians were
famous for going to Harlem and other Negro cultural
centers literally to steal the black man's music, carrying it
back across the color line into the Great White World and
passing off the watered-down loot as their own original
creations. Blacks, meanwhile, were ridiculed as *Negro* musicians playing inferior coon music.

The Negro revolution at home and national liberation
movements abroad have unceremoniously shattered the
world of fantasy in which the whites have been living. It is
painful that many do not yet see that their fantasy world
has been rendered uninhabitable in the last half of the
twentieth century. But it is away from this world that the
white youth of today are turning. The "paper tiger" hero,
James Bond, offering the whites a triumphant image of
themselves, is saying what many whites want desperately to
hear reaffirmed: *I am still the White Man, lord of the land,
licensed to kill, and the world is still an empire at my feet.*
James Bond feeds on that secret little anxiety, the psychological white backlash, felt in some degree by most whites
alive. It is exasperating to see little brown men and little
yellow men from the mysterious Orient, and the opaque
black men of Africa (to say nothing of these impudent
American Negroes!) who come to the UN and talk smart to
us, who are scurrying all over *our* globe in their strange

modes of dress—much as if they were new, unpleasant arrivals from another planet. Many whites believe in their ulcers that it is only a matter of time before the Marines get the signal to round up these truants and put them back securely in their cages. But it is away from this fantasy world that the white youth of today are turning.

In the world revolution now under way, the initiative rests with people of color. That growing numbers of white youth are repudiating their heritage of blood and taking people of color as their heroes and models is a tribute not only to their insight but to the resilience of the human spirit. For today the heroes of the initiative are people not usually thought of as white: Fidel Castro, Che Guevara, Kwame Nkrumah, Mao Tse-tung, Gamal Abdel Nasser, Robert F. Williams, Malcolm X, Ben Bella, John Lewis, Martin Luther King, Jr., Robert Parris Moses, Ho Chi Minh, Stokeley Carmichael, W. E. B. DuBois, James Forman, Chou En-lai.

The white youth of today have begun to react to the fact that the "American Way of Life" is a fossil of history. What do they care if their old baldheaded and crew-cut elders don't dig their caveman mops? They couldn't care less about the old, stiffassed honkies who don't like their new dances: Frug, Monkey, Jerk, Swim, Watusi. All they know is that it feels good to swing to way-out body-rhythms instead of dragassing across the dance floor like zombies to the dead beat of mind-smothered Mickey Mouse music. Is it any wonder that the youth have lost all respect for their elders, for law and order, when for as long as they can remember all they've witnessed is a monumental bickering over the Negro's place in American society and the right of people around the world to be left alone by outside powers? They have witnessed the law, both domestic and international, being spat upon by those who do not like its terms. Is it any wonder, then, that they feel justified, by sitting-in and freedom riding, in breaking laws made by lawless men? Old funny-styled, zipper-mouthed political night riders know nothing but to haul out an investigating committee *to look into the disturbance* to find the cause of the unrest among the youth. Look into a mirror! The cause is you, Mr. and Mrs. Yesterday, you with your forked tongues.

A young white today cannot help but recoil from the base deeds of his people. On every side, on every continent, he sees racial arrogance, savage brutality toward the conquered and subjugated people, genocide; he sees the human cargo of the slave trade; he sees the systematic extermination of American Indians; he sees the civilized nations of Europe fighting in imperial depravity over the lands of other people—and over possession of the very people themselves. There seems to be no end to the ghastly deeds of which his people are guilty. *GUILTY*. The slaughter of the Jews by the Germans, the dropping of atomic bombs on the Japanese people—these deeds weigh heavily upon the prostrate souls and tumultuous consciences of the white youth. The white heroes, their hands dripping with blood, are dead.

The young whites know that the colored people of the world, Afro-Americans included, do not seek revenge for their suffering. They seek the same things the white rebel wants: an end to war and exploitation. Black and white, the young rebels are free people, free in a way that Americans have never been before in the history of their country. And they are outraged.

There is in America today a generation of white youth that is truly worthy of a black man's respect, and this is a rare event in the foul annals of American history. From the beginning of the contact between blacks and whites, there has been very little reason for a black man to respect a

white, with such exceptions as John Brown and others
lesser known. But respect commands itself and it can
neither be given nor withheld when it is due. If a man like
Malcolm X could change and repudiate racism, if I myself
and other former Muslims can change, if young whites can
change, then there is hope for America. It was certainly
strange to find myself, while steeped in the doctrine that all
whites were devils by nature, commanded by the heart to
applaud and acknowledge respect for these young whites
—despite the fact that they are descendants of the masters
and I the descendant of slave. The sins of the fathers are
visited upon the heads of the children—but only if the children continue in the evil deeds of the fathers.

Lazarus, Come Forth

The Blood Lust

The boxing ring is the ultimate focus of masculinity in America, the two-fisted testing ground of manhood, and the heavyweight champion, as a symbol, is the real Mr. America. In a culture that secretly subscribes to the piratical ethic of "every man for himself"—the social Darwinism of "survival of the fittest" being far from dead, manifesting itself in our ratrace political system of competing parties, in our dog-eat-dog economic system of profit and loss, and in our adversary system of justice wherein truth is secondary to the skill and connections of the advocate—the logical culmination of this ethic, on a person-to-person level, is that the weak are seen as the natural and just prey of the strong. But since this dark principle violates our democratic ideals and professions, we force it underground, out of a perverse national modesty that reveals us as a nation of peep freaks who prefer the bikini to the naked body, the white lie to the black truth, Hollywood smiles and canned laughter to a soulful Bronx cheer. The heretical mailed fist of American reality rises to the surface in the velvet glove of our every institutionalized endeavor, so that each year we, as a nation, grind through various cycles of attrition, symbolically quenching the insatiable appetite of the *de facto* jungle law underlying our culture, loudly and unabashedly proclaiming to the world that "competition" is the law of life,

84

getting confused, embarrassed, and angry if someone re-
torts: "Competition is the Law of the Jungle and Coopera-
tion is the Law of Civilization."

Our mass spectator sports are geared to disguise, while
affording expression to, the acting out in elaborate pageant-
ry of the myth of the fittest in the process of surviving.
From the Little League to the major leagues, through the
orgiastic climax of the World Series; from high school
football teams, through the college teams, to the grand
finale of the annual bowl washouts; interspersed with the
subcycles of basketball, track, and field meets—all of our
mass spectator sports give play to the basic cultural ethic,
harnessed and sublimated into national-communal pagan
rituals.

But there is an aspect of the crystal of our nature that
eschews the harness, scorns sublimation, and demands to be
seen in its raw nakedness, crying out to us for the sight and
smell of blood. The vehemence with which we deny this
obvious fact of our nature is matched only by our Vic-
torian hysteria on the subject of sex. Yet, we deny it
in vain. Whether we quench our thirst from the
sight of a bleeding Jesus on the Cross, from the
ritualized sacrifice in the elevation of the Host and the
consecration of the Blood of the Son, or from bullfight-
ing, cockfighting, dogfighting, wrestling, or boxing, spiced
with our Occidental memory and heritage of the gladiators
of Rome and the mass spectator sport of the time of feeding
Christians and other enemies of society to the lions in the
Coliseum—whatever the mask assumed by the impulse, the
persistent beat of the drum over the years intones the chant:
Though Dracula and Vampira must flee the scene with the
rising of the sun and the coming of the light, night has its
fixed hour and darkness must fall. And all the lightbulbs
ever fashioned, and all the power plants generating elec-

tricity, have absolutely no effect on the primeval spinning of the earth in its orbit.

In America, we give maximum expression to our blood lust in the mass spectator sport of boxing. Some of us are Roman enough to admit our love and need of the sport. Others pretend to look the other way. But when a heavy-weight championship fight rolls around, the nation takes a moral holiday and we are all tuned in—some of us peeping out of the corner of our eye at the square jungle and the animal test of brute power unfolding there.

Every institution in America is tainted by the mystique of race, and the question of masculinity is confused by the presence of both a "white" man and a "black" man here. One was the master and the other was the slave until a moment ago when they both were declared to be equal "men"; which leaves American men literally without a unitary, nationally viable self-image. Whatever dim vision of masculinity they have is a rough-and-ready, savage mishmash of violence and sexuality, a dichotomized exer-cise and worship of physical force/submission to and fear of physical force—which is only one aspect of the broken-down relationship between men and women in America. This is an era when the models of manhood and woman-hood have been blasted to dust by social upheaval, as the most alienated males and females at the bottom of society move out of "their places" and bid for their right to be "man" and "woman" on an equal basis with the former masters and mistresses. These, in turn, are no longer seen by themselves and others as supermen and superwomen, but only as men and women like all other. And in this period of social change and sexual confusion, boxing, and the heavyweight championship in particular, serves as the ultimate test of masculinity, based on the perfection of the body and its use.

The Negro Celebrity

The murder of Malcolm X, the exile of Robert F. Williams, who was forced to flee to Cuba with the combined terrors of the FBI and the minions of Southern justice snapping at his heels, and the exile of the late W. E. B. DuBois, who, in the sunset of a valiant life, made three symbolic gestures as a final legacy to his people (renouncing his American citizenship, "returning" to Africa to become a citizen of Ghana, and cursing capitalism while extolling communism as the hope of the future)—these events on the one hand, and on the other hand the award of a Nobel Prize to Martin Luther King and the inflation of his image to that of an international hero, bear witness to the historical fact that the only Negro Americans allowed to attain national or international fame have been the puppets and lackeys of the white power structure—and entertainers and athletes.

One tactic by which the rulers of America have kept the bemused millions of Negroes in optimum subjugation has been a conscious, systematic emasculation of Negro leadership. Through an elaborate system of sanctions, rewards, penalties, and persecutions—with, more often than not, members of the black bourgeoisie acting as hatchet men— any Negro who sought leadership over the black masses and refused to become a tool of the white power structure was either cast into prison, killed, hounded out of the country, or blasted into obscurity and isolation in his own land and among his own people. His isolation was assured by publicity boycotts alternated with character assassination in the mass media, and by the fratricidal power plays of Uncle Toms who control the Negro community on behalf of the white power structure. The classic illustrations of this quash-the-black-militant policy are the careers of Marcus Garvey, W. E. B. DuBois, and Paul Robeson.

Garvey, who in the first quarter of this century sparked a black mass movement based in America but international in scope and potential, was cast into federal prison and then exiled to England. W. E. B. DuBois, one of the intellectual giants of the modern world, was silenced and isolated in America as viciously and effectively as the racist regime in South Africa has silenced and isolated such leaders of the black masses as Chief Albert Luthuli, or as the British, in Kenya, once silenced and isolated Jomo Kenyatta. After attempts to cast him into prison on trumped-up charges had failed, DuBois went into exile in Ghana and later renounced the bitter citizenship of the land of his birth.

Paul Robeson was at the apex of an illustrious career as a singer and actor, earning over $200,000 a year, when he began speaking out passionately in behalf of his people, unable to balance the luxury of his own life with the squalor of the black masses from which he sprang and of which he was proud. The response of the black masses to his charisma alarmed both the Uncle Toms and the white power structure, and Paul Robeson was marked for destruction. Through a coordinated, sustained effort, Robeson became the object of economic boycott and character assassination. Broken financially, and heartbroken to see black Uncle Toms working assiduously to defeat him and keep their own people down, Robeson's spirit was crushed, his health subverted, and his career destroyed.

By crushing black leaders, while inflating the images of Uncle Toms and celebrities from the apolitical world of sport and play, the mass media were able to channel and control the aspirations and goals of the black masses. The effect was to take the "problem" out of a political and economic and philosophical context and place it on the misty level of "goodwill," "charitable and harmonious race relations," and "good sportsmanlike conduct." This technique of "Negro control" has been so effective that the best-known Negroes in America have always been—and still are—the entertainers and athletes (this is true also of white America). The tradition is that whenever a crisis with racial overtones arises, an entertainer or athlete is trotted out and allowed to expound a predictable, conciliatory interpretation of what's happening. The mass media rush forward with grinding cameras and extended microphones as though some great oracle were about to lay down a new covenant from God; when in reality, all that has happened is that the blacks have been sold out and cooled out again—*"One more time, boom! One more time, boom!"*

When the question of segregation in the armed services arose during the '40s, the then heavyweight champion of the world, Joe Louis, and Louis Satchmo Armstrong, who was also noted for blowing a trumpet, were more likely to be quoted on the subject than A. Philip Randolph or W. E. B. DuBois. And more recently, at the peak of a nationwide epidemic of sit-ins and demonstrations, Attorney General Robert Kennedy called together a group of "influential" Negro entertainers and athletes to meet with him in secret, to get the message from The Man and carry the gospel back to the restless natives. It actually seemed possible to this intelligent Enforcer of the Establishment Will that Queen of the Mellow Mood, Lena Horne, and Harry Belafonte, quarterbacked by James Baldwin, were qualified—not to say "willing," which they weren't—to say or do something to make the black and white hordes of insurgents "freeze" for a cooling-off period. Obviously, the move made sense to Kennedy. It was worth trying, because Kennedy knew that it was based on a solid tradition which had worked for years. But times had changed, fundamentally, and Kennedy's attempted cool-out was greeted with hoots of scorn and contempt from Negroes—entertainers and athletes included. Just as funnyman Dick Gregory got himself shot trying to "cool off" revolting Negroes in Watts, the celebrities knew that their standing in the black community, which suddenly had become important to them, could easily be destroyed if the impression got out that they were cooperating in an Uncle Tom cool-out this late in the game. The stakes were growing higher, and Negroes everywhere were becoming eager and anxious to bet their lives against the *status quo*. The stupidity of the Uncle Tom cool-out reached perhaps its most grotesque incarnation when, after Negroes had rioted and burned in Harlem, the black friends of the white power structure issued a pamphlet with the headline COOL IT, BABY!

But proof that the power structure never learns can be found in the ludicrous action of the wheels within wheels who rule Los Angeles. After the biggest, most violent Negro uprising since the Civil War—the burning of Watts —the blind, tradition-bound reactionaries of L.A. sought to placate the aroused Negro community by appointing John Roseboro, a baseball player, "ace catcher for the Los Angeles Dodgers," to the position of consultant on community relations. One of his tasks being to spread "goodwill" between Negroes and Chief Parker's Police Department!

It is against this background—of the traditional role of the Negro entertainer and athlete in racial crisis and the rebellion against that tradition—that the Muhammad Ali–Floyd Patterson fight for the world heavyweight championship must be viewed.

The Muhammad Ali–Patterson Fight

It is tempting to say that the Muhammad Ali–Floyd Patterson fight was an "internal affair" of the Negro people. But how could that be, if it is true that both fighters and the boxing game itself, like everything else in America, are more or less owned and controlled by whites? The fight was, ideologically, a pivotal event, reflecting the consolidation of certain psychic gains of the Negro revolution. However, the diplomatic fiction of the "internal affair," no longer operative in international politics, is also inoperative here. Both black and white America, looking on, were sucked into the vortex of the event, feeling somehow a profound relationship to what was being enacted in that ring. They knew that a triumph and a defeat were taking place with consequences for America, transcending the fortunes of the two men squaring off in the ring to test their strength.

The simplistic version of the fight bandied about in the press was that there was a "white hope" and a "black hope" riding on this fight. The white hope for a Patterson victory was, in essence, a counterrevolutionary desire to force the Negro, now in rebellion and personified in the boxing world by Ali, back into his "place." The black hope, on the contrary, was to see Lazarus crushed, to see Uncle Tom defeated, to be given symbolic proof of the victory of the autonomous Negro over the subordinate Negro.

The broad support for Muhammad Ali among Negroes had nothing to do with the black Muslims' racist ideology. Even the followers of the late beloved Malcolm X, many of whom despise Muhammad Ali for the scurvy remarks he made about the fallen Malcolm, nevertheless favored him over Patterson as the lesser of two evils—because Ali was more in harmony with the furious psychic stance of the Negro today, while Patterson was an anachronism light years behind. In time of war, in the very center of the battle, the man of peace cannot command the ear of his people and he loses ground to the man of war. The revolutionary rage in the black man's soul today, which boiled over and burned Watts to the ground, means nothing if it doesn't mean business, and it was focused in cold, deadly hatred and contempt upon Floyd Patterson and the bootlicking art of the puppet in the style of his image.

There is no doubt that white America will accept a black champion, applaud and reward him, as long as there is no "white hope" in sight. But what white America demands in her black champions is a brilliant, powerful body and a dull, bestial mind—a tiger in the ring and a pussycat outside the ring. It is a hollow, cruel mockery to crown a man king in the boxing ring and then shove him about outside, going so far as to burn a cross on his front doorstep, as whites did when Floyd Patterson tried to integrate a neighborhood. "A man's home is his castle" is a saying not meant for Negroes; a Negro's castle exists only in his mind. And for a black king of boxing the boundaries of his kingdom are sharply circumscribed by the ropes around the ring. A slave in private life, a king in public—this is the life that every black champion has had to lead—until the coming of Muhammad Ali.

Muhammad Ali is the first "free" black champion ever to confront white America. In the context of boxing, he is a genuine revolutionary, the black Fidel Castro of boxing. To the mind of "white" white America, and "white" black America, the heavyweight crown has fallen into enemy hands, usurped by a pretender to the throne. Muhammad Ali is conceived as "occupying" the heavyweight kingdom in the name of a dark, alien power, in much the same way as Castro was conceived as a temporary interloper "occupying" Cuba. It made no difference that, when Patterson announced that he would beat Ali and return the crown to America, Ali protested vigorously, asking, "What does he mean? I'm an American too!" Floyd Patterson was the symbolic spearhead of a counterrevolutionary host, leader of the mythical legions of faithful darkies who inhabit the white imagination, whose assigned task it was to liberate the crown and restore it to its proper "place" in the Free World. Muhammad Ali, in crushing the Rabbit in twelve —after punishing him at will so there could be no doubt, so that the sports writers could not rob him of his victory on paper—inflicted a psychological chastisement on "white" white America similar in shock value to Fidel Castro's at the Bay of Pigs. If the Bay of Pigs can be seen as a straight right hand to the psychological jaw of white America, then Las Vegas was a perfect left hook to the gut.

Essentially, every black champion until Muhammad Ali has been a puppet, manipulated by whites in his private life to control his public image. His role was to conceal the strings from which he was suspended, so as to appear autonomous and self-motivated before the public. But with the coming of Muhammad Ali, the puppet-master was left with a handful of strings to which his dancing doll was no longer attached. For every white man, feeling himself superior to every black man, it was a serious blow to his self-image; because Muhammad Ali, by the very fact that he leads an autonomous private life, cannot fulfill the psychological needs of whites.

The heavyweight champion is a symbol of masculinity to the American male. And a black champion, as long as he is firmly fettered in his private life, is a fallen lion at every white man's feet. Through a curious psychic mechanism, the puniest white man experiences himself as a giant-killer, as a superman, a great white hunter leading a gigantic ape, the black champion tamed by the white man, around on a leash. But when the ape breaks away from the leash, beats with deadly fists upon his massive chest and starts talking to boot, proclaiming himself to be the greatest, spouting poetry, and annihilating every gunbearer the white hunter sics on him (the white hunter not being disposed to crawl into the ring himself), a very serious slippage takes place in the white man's self-image—*because that by which he defined himself no longer has a recognizable identity.* "If that black ape is a man," the white hunter asks himself, "then what am I?"

It was really Sonny Liston who marked the coming of the autonomous Negro to boxing. But he was nonideological and so the scandal he caused could be handled, albeit with difficulty and pain. The mystique he exuded was that of a lone wolf who did not belong to his people or speak for them. He was for Liston and spoke only for Liston, and this was not out of harmony with the competitive ethic undergirding American culture. If every man is for himself, it was rational for Liston to be for *him*self. Although even this degree of autonomy in a Negro was bitterly resented, white America could tolerate it with less hysteria, with less of a sense of being threatened. But when the ideological Negro seized the heavyweight crown, no front of cool could conceal the ferocious emotional eruption in white America and among the embarrassed Uncle Toms, who were also experiencing an identity crisis. Yes, even old faithful Uncle Tom has a self-image. All men must have one or they start seeing themselves as women, women start seeing them as women, then women lose their own self-image, and soon nobody knows what they are themselves or what anyone else is—that is to say, the world starts looking precisely as it looks today. For there to be so deep an uproar over Muhammad Ali should indicate that there is something much more serious than a boxing title at stake, something cutting right to the center of the madness of our time.

The New Testament parable of Jesus raising Lazarus from the dead is interpreted by the Black Muslims as a symbolic parallel to the history of the Negro in America. By capturing black men in Africa and bringing them to slavery in America, the white devils *killed* the black man—killed him mentally, culturally, spiritually, economically, politically, and morally—transforming him into a "Negro," the symbolic Lazarus left in the "graveyard" of segregation and second-class citizenship. And just as Jesus was summoned to the cave to raise Lazarus from the dead, Elijah Muhammad had been summoned by God to lift up the modern Lazarus, the Negro, from his grave.

"Come out of her, my people!" cries Elijah Muhammad.

Cassius Clay, shedding his graveyard identity like an old dead skin, is one who heeded Elijah's call, repudiating the identity America gave him and taking on a new identity— Muhammad Ali. Floyd Patterson did not heed Elijah.

The America out of which Elijah Muhammad calls his people is indeed doomed, crumbling, burning, if not by the hand of God then by the hand of man, and this doomed America was partly buried in the boxing ring at Las Vegas when Muhammad Ali pounded a die-hard Lazarus into submission. With the America that is disappearing, the Lazarus-man created in the crucible of its hatred and pain is also vanishing. The victory of Muhammad Ali over Floyd Patterson marks the victory of a New World over an Old World, of life and light over Lazarus and the darkness of the grave. This is America recreating itself out of its own ruins. The pain is mighty for every American, black or white, because the task is gigantic and by no means certain of fulfillment. But there are strong men in this land and they will not be denied. Their task will not be ended until both Paul Bunyan and John Henry can look upon themselves and each other as men, the strength in the image of the one not being at the expense of the other.

Harsh, brutal, and vicious though it may be, no one can deny Muhammad Ali his triumph, and though you comb

the ghettos of your desperate cities and beat the bushes of
your black belts for another puppet who will succeed where
the Rabbit failed, your search will be in vain. Because even
as you search you, yourself, are being changed, and you
will understand that you must continue to change or die.
Yes, the Louisville Lip is a loudmouthed braggart. Yes, he
is a Black Muslim racist, staunch enough in the need of his
beliefs to divorce his wife for not adopting his religion; and
firing his trainer, who taught him to "float like a butterfly
and sting like a bee," for the same reason. But he is also a
"free" man, determined not to be a white man's puppet
even though he fights to entertain them; determined to be
autonomous in his private life and a true king of his realm
in public, and he is exactly that. A racist Black Muslim
heavyweight champion is a bitter pill for racist white
America to swallow. Swallow it—or throw the whole bit
up, and hope that in the convulsions of your guts, America,
you can vomit out the poisons of hate which have led you to
a dead end in this valley of the shadow of death.

Notes on a Native Son

After reading a couple of James Baldwin's books, I began experiencing that continuous delight one feels upon discovering a fascinating, brilliant talent on the scene, a talent capable of penetrating so profoundly into one's own little world that one knows oneself to have been unalterably changed and *liberated,* liberated from the frustrating grasp of whatever devils happen to possess one. Being a Negro, I have found this to be a rare and infrequent experience, for few of my black brothers and sisters here in America have achieved the power, which James Baldwin calls his revenge, which outlasts kingdoms: the power of doing whatever cats like Baldwin do when combining the alphabet with the volatile elements of his soul. (And, like it or not, a black man, unless he has become irretrievably "white-minded," responds with an additional dimension of his being to the articulated experience of another black—in spite of the universality of human experience.)

I, as I imagine many others did and still do, lusted for anything that Baldwin had written. It would have been a gas for me to sit on a pillow beneath the womb of Baldwin's typewriter and catch each newborn page as it entered this world of ours. I was delighted that Baldwin, with those great big eyes of his, which one thought to be fixedly focused on the macrocosm, could also pierce the microcosm.

And although he was so full of sound, he was not a noisy writer like Ralph Ellison. He placed so much of my own experience, which I thought I had understood, into new perspective.

Gradually, however, I began to feel uncomfortable about something in Baldwin. I was disturbed upon becoming aware of an aversion in my heart to part of the song he sang. Why this was so, I was unable at first to say. Then I read *Another Country,* and I knew why my love for Baldwin's vision had become ambivalent.

Long before, I had become a student of Norman Mailer's *The White Negro,* which seemed to me to be prophetic and penetrating in its understanding of the psychology involved in the accelerating confrontation of black and white in America. I was therefore personally insulted by Baldwin's flippant, schoolmarmish dismissal of *The White Negro.* Baldwin committed a literary crime by his arrogant repudiation of one of the few gravely important expressions of our time. *The White Negro* may contain an excess of esoteric verbal husk, but one can forgive Mailer for that because of the solid kernel of truth he gave us. After all, it is the baby we want and not the blood of afterbirth. Mailer described, in that incisive essay, the first important chinks in the "mountain of white supremacy"—important because it shows the depth of ferment, on a personal level, in the white world. People are feverishly, and at great psychic and social expense, seeking *fundamental and irrevocable liberation*— and, what is more important, *are succeeding in escaping*— from the big white lies that compose the monolithic myth of White Supremacy/Black Inferiority, in a desperate attempt on the part of a new generation of white Americans to enter into the cosmopolitan egalitarian spirit of the twentieth century. But let us examine the reasoning that lies behind Baldwin's attack on Mailer.

There is in James Baldwin's work the most grueling, agonizing, total hatred of the blacks, particularly of himself, and the most shameful, fanatical, fawning, sycophantic love of the whites that one can find in the writings of any black American writer of note in our time. This is an appalling contradiction and the implications of it are vast.

A rereading of *Nobody Knows My Name* cannot help but convince the most avid of Baldwin's admirers of the hatred for blacks permeating his writings. In the essay "Princes and Powers," Baldwin's antipathy toward the black race is shockingly clear. The essay is Baldwin's interpretation of the Conference of Black Writers and Artists which met in Paris in September 1956. The portrait of Baldwin that comes through his words is that of a mind in unrelenting opposition to the efforts of solemn, dedicated black men who have undertaken the enormous task of rejuvenating and reclaiming the shattered psyches and culture of the black people, a people scattered over the continents of the world and the islands of the seas, where they exist in the mud of the floor of the foul dungeon into which the world has been transformed by the whites.

In his report of the conference, Baldwin, the reluctant black, dragging his feet at every step, could only ridicule the vision and efforts of these great men and heap scorn upon them, reserving his compliments—all of them left-handed—for the speakers at the conference who were themselves rejected and booed by the other conferees because of their reactionary, sycophantic views. Baldwin felt called upon to pop his cap pistol in a duel with Aimé Césaire, the big gun from Martinique. Indirectly, Baldwin was defending his first love—the white man. But the revulsion which Baldwin felt for the blacks at this conference, who were glorying in their blackness, seeking and showing their pride in Negritude and the African Personality, drives him to self-revealing sortie after sortie, so obvious in "Princes and Powers." Each successive sortie, however, becomes more expensive than the last one, because to score each time he has to go a little farther out on the limb, and it takes him a little longer each time to hustle back to the cover and camouflage of the perfumed smoke screen of his prose. Now and then we catch a glimpse of his little jive ass—his big eyes peering back over his shoulder in the mischievous retreat of a child sneak-thief from a cookie jar.

In the autobiographical notes of *Notes of a Native Son,* Baldwin is frank to confess that, in growing into his version of manhood in Harlem, he discovered that, since his African heritage had been wiped out and was not accessible to him, he would appropriate the white man's heritage and make it his own. This terrible reality, central to the psychic stance of all American Negroes, revealed to Baldwin that he hated and feared white people. Then he says: "This did not mean that I loved black people; on the contrary, I despised them, possibly because they failed to produce Rembrandt." The psychic distance between love and hate could be the mechanical difference between a smile and a sneer, or it could be the journey of a nervous impulse from the depths of one's brain to the tip of one's toe. But this impulse in its path through North American nerves may, if it is honest, find the passage disputed: may find the leap from the fiber of hate to that of love too taxing on its meager store of energy—and so the long trip back may never be completed, may end in a reconnaissance, a compromise, and then a lie.

Self-hatred takes many forms; sometimes it can be detected by no one, not by the keenest observer, not by the self-hater himself, not by his most intimate friends. Ethnic self-hate is even more difficult to detect. But in American

Negroes, this ethnic self-hatred often takes the bizarre form of a racial death-wish, with many and elusive manifestations. Ironically, it provides much of the impetus behind the motivations of integration. And the attempt to suppress or deny such drives in one's psyche leads many American Negroes to become ostentatious separationists, Black Muslims, and back-to-Africa advocates. It is no wonder that Elijah Muhammad could conceive of the process of controlling evolution whereby the white race was brought into being. According to Elijah, about 6300 years ago all the people of the earth were Original Blacks. Secluded on the island of Patmos, a mad black scientist by the name of Yacub set up the machinery for grafting whites out of blacks through the operation of a birth-control system. The population on this island of Patmos was 59,999 and whenever a couple on this island wanted to get married they were only allowed to do so if there was a difference in their color, so that by mating black with those in the population of a brownish color and brown with brown—but never black with black—all traces of the black were eventually eliminated; the process was repeated until all the brown was eliminated, leaving only men of the red race; the red was bleached out, leaving only yellow; then the yellow was bleached out, and only white was left. Thus Yacub, who was long since dead, because this whole process took hundreds of years, had finally succeeded in creating the white devil with the blue eyes of death.

This myth of the creation of the white race, called "Yacub's History," is an inversion of the racial death-wish of American Negroes. Yacub's plan is still being followed by many Negroes today. Quite simply, many Negroes believe, as the principle of assimilation into white America implies, that the race problem in America cannot be settled until all traces of the black race are eliminated. Toward this end, many Negroes loathe the very idea of two very dark Negroes mating. The children, they say, will come out ugly. What they mean is that the children are sure to be black, and this is not desirable. From the widespread use of cosmetics to bleach the black out of one's skin and other concoctions to take Africa out of one's hair, to the extreme, resorted to by more Negroes than one might wish to believe, of undergoing nose-thinning and lip-clipping operations, the racial death-wish of American Negroes—Yacub's goal—takes its terrible toll. What has been happening for the past four hundred years is that the white man, through his access to black women, has been pumping his blood and genes into the blacks, has been diluting the blood and genes of the blacks—i.e., has been fulfilling Yacub's plan and accelerating the Negroes' racial death-wish.

The case of James Baldwin aside for a moment, it seems that many Negro homosexuals, acquiescing in this racial death-wish, are outraged and frustrated because in their sickness they are unable to have a baby by a white man. The cross they have to bear is that, already bending over and touching their toes for the white man, the fruit of their miscegenation is not the little half-white offspring of their dreams but an increase in the unwinding of their nerves— though they redouble their efforts and intake of the white man's sperm.

In this land of dichotomies and disunited opposites, those truly concerned with the resurrection of black Americans have had eternally to deal with black intellectuals who have become their own opposites, taking on all of the behavior patterns of their enemy, vices and virtues, in an effort to aspire to alien standards in all respects. The gulf between an audacious, bootlicking Uncle Tom and an intellectual buckdancer is filled only with sophistication and style. On second thought, Uncle Tom comes off much cleaner here because usually he is just trying to survive, choosing to pretend to be something other than his true self in order to please the white man and thus receive favors. Whereas the intellectual sycophant does not pretend to be other than he actually is, but hates what he is and seeks to redefine himself in the image of his white idols. He becomes a white man in a black body. A self-willed, automated slave, he becomes the white man's most valuable tool in oppressing other blacks.

The black homosexual, when his twist has a racial nexus, is an extreme embodiment of this contradiction. The white man has deprived him of his masculinity, castrated him in the center of his burning skull, and when he submits to this change and takes the white man for his lover as well as Big Daddy, he focuses on "whiteness" all the love in his pent up soul and turns the razor edge of hatred against "blackness"—upon himself, what he is, and all those who look like him, remind him of himself. He may even hate the darkness of night.

The racial death-wish is manifested as the driving force in James Baldwin. His hatred for blacks, even as he pleads what he conceives as their cause, makes him the apotheosis of the dilemma in the ethos of the black bourgeoisie who have completely rejected their African heritage, consider the loss irrevocable, and refuse to look again in that direction. This is the root of Baldwin's violent repudiation of Mailer's *The White Negro*.

To understand what is at stake here, and to understand it in terms of the life of this nation, is to know the central fact that the relationship between black and white in America is a power equation, a power struggle, and that this power struggle is not only manifested in the aggregate (civil rights, black nationalism, etc.) but also in the interpersonal relationships, actions, and reactions between blacks and whites where taken into account. When those "two lean cats," Baldwin and Mailer, met in a French living room, it was precisely this power equation that was at work.

It is fascinating to read (in *Nobody Knows My Name*) in what terms this power equation was manifested in Baldwin's immediate reaction to that meeting: "And here we were, suddenly, circling around each other. We liked each other at once, but each was frightened that the other would pull rank. He could have pulled rank on me because he was more famous and *had more money* and also *because he was white;* but I could have pulled rank on him precisely because I was black and knew more about that periphery he so helplessly maligns in *The White Negro* than he could ever hope to know." [Italics added.]

Pulling rank, it would seem, is a very dangerous business, especially when the troops have mutinied and the basis of one's authority, or rank, is devoid of that interdictive power and has become suspect. One would think that for Baldwin, of all people, these hues of black and white were no longer armed with the power to intimidate—and if one thought this, one would be exceedingly wrong: for behind the structure of the thought of Baldwin's quoted above, there lurks the imp of Baldwin's unwinding, of his tension between love and hate—love of the white and hate of the black. And when we dig into this tension we will find that when those "two lean cats" crossed tracks in that French living room, one was a Pussy Cat, the other a Tiger. Baldwin's purr was transmitted magnificently in *The Fire Next Time.* But his work is the fruit of a tree with a poison root. Such succulent fruit, such a painful tree, what a malignant root!

It is ironic, but fascinating for what it reveals about the

ferment in the North American soul in our time, that Norman Mailer, the white boy, and James Baldwin, the black boy, encountered each other in the eye of a social storm, traveling in opposite directions; the white boy, with knowledge of white Negroes, was traveling toward a confrontation with the black, with Africa; while the black boy, with a white mind, was on his way to Europe. Baldwin's nose, like the North-seeking needle on a compass, is forever pointed toward his adopted fatherland, Europe, his by intellectual osmosis and in Africa's stead. What he says of Aimé Césaire, one of the greatest black writers of the twentieth century, and intending it as an ironic rebuke, that "he had penetrated into the heart of the great wilderness which was Europe and stolen the sacred fire . . . which . . . was . . . the assurance of his power," seems only too clearly to speak more about Peter than it does about Paul. What Baldwin seems to forget is that Césaire explains that fire, whether sacred or profane, burns. In Baldwin's case, though the fire could not burn the black off his face, it certainly did burn it out of his heart.

I am not interested in denying anything to Baldwin. I, like the entire nation, owe a great debt to him. But throughout the range of his work, from *Go Tell It on the Mountain,* through *Notes of a Native Son, Nobody Knows My Name, Another Country,* to *The Fire Next Time,* all of which I treasure, there is a decisive quirk in Baldwin's vision which corresponds to his relationship to black people and to masculinity. It was this same quirk, in my opinion, that compelled Baldwin to slander Rufus Scott in *Another Country,* venerate André Gide, repudiate *The White Negro,* and drive the blade of Brutus into the corpse of Richard Wright. As Baldwin has said in *Nobody Knows My Name,* "I think that I know something about the American masculinity which most men of my generation do not know because they have not been menaced by it in the way I have been." O.K., Sugar, but isn't it true that Rufus Scott, the weak, craven-hearted ghost of *Another Country,* bears the same relation to Bigger Thomas of *Native Son,* the black rebel of the ghetto and a man, as you yourself bore to the fallen giant, Richard Wright, a rebel and a man?

Somewhere in one of his books, Richard Wright describes an encounter between a ghost and several young Negroes. The young Negroes rejected the homosexual, and this was Wright alluding to a classic, if cruel, example of a ubiquitous phenomenon in the black ghettos of America: the practice by Negro youths of going "punk-hunting." This practice of seeking out homosexuals on the prowl, rolling them, beating them up, seemingly just to satisfy some savage impulse to inflict pain on the specific target selected, the "social outcast," seems to me to be not unrelated, in terms of the psychological mechanisms involved, to the ritualistic lynchings and castrations inflicted on Southern blacks by Southern whites. This was, as I recall, one of Wright's few comments on the subject of homosexuality.

I think it can safely be said that the men in Wright's books, albeit shackled with a form of impotence, were strongly heterosexual. Their heterosexuality was implied rather than laboriously stated or emphasized; it was taken for granted, as we all take men until something occurs to make us know otherwise. And Bigger Thomas, Wright's greatest creation, was a man in violent, though inept, rebellion against the stifling, murderous, totalitarian white world. There was no trace in Bigger of a Martin Luther King-type self-effacing love for his oppressors. For example, Bigger would have been completely baffled, as most Negroes are today, at Baldwin's advice to his nephew (*The Fire Next Time*), concerning white people: "You must accept them *and accept them with love.* For these innocent people have no other hope." [Italics added.]

Rufus Scott, a pathetic wretch who indulged in the white man's pastime of committing suicide, who let a white bisexual homosexual fuck him in his ass, and who took a Southern Jezebel for his woman, with all that these tortured relationships imply, was the epitome of a black eunuch who has completely submitted to the white man. Yes, Rufus was a psychological freedom rider, turning the ultimate cheek, murmuring like a ghost, *"You took the best so why not take the rest,"* which has absolutely nothing to do with the way Negroes have managed to survive here in the hells of North America! This all becomes very clear from what we learn of Erich, the arch-ghost of *Another Country,* of the depths of his alienation from his body and the source of his need: "And it had taken him almost until this very moment, on the eve of his departure, to begin to recognize that part of Rufus' great power over him had to do with the past which Erich had buried in some deep, dark place; was connected with himself, in Alabama, *when I wasn't nothing but a child;* with the cold white people and the warm black people, warm at least for him. . . ."

So, too, who cannot wonder at the source of such audacious madness as moved Baldwin to make this startling remark about Richard Wright, in his ignoble essay "Alas, Poor Richard": "In my own relations with him, I was always exasperated by his notions of society, politics, and history, for they seemed to me utterly fanciful. I never believed that he had any real sense of how a society is put together."

Richard Wright is dead and Baldwin is alive and with us. Baldwin says that Richard Wright held notions that were utterly fanciful, and Baldwin is an honorable man.

> *"O judgment; thou art fled to*
> *brutish beasts,*
> *And men have lost their reason!"*

Wright has no need, as Caesar did, of an outraged Antony to plead his cause: his life and his work are his shield against the mellow thrust of Brutus' blade. The good that he did, unlike Caesar's, will not be interred with his bones. It is, on the contrary, only the living who can be harmed by Brutus.

Baldwin says that in Wright's writings violence sits enthroned where sex should be. If this is so, then it is only because in the North American reality hate holds sway in love's true province. And it is only through a rank perversion that the artist, whose duty is to tell us the truth, can turn the two-dollar trick of wedding violence to love and sex to hate—if, to achieve this end, one has basely to transmute rebellion into lamblike submission—*"You took the best,"* sniveled Rufus, *"so why not take the rest?"* Richard Wright was not ghost enough to achieve this cruel distortion. With him, sex, being not a spectator sport or a panacea but the sacred vehicle of life and love, is itself sacred. And the America which Wright knew and which *is,* is not the Garden of Eden but its opposite. Baldwin, embodying in his art the self-flagellating policy of Martin Luther King, and giving out falsely the news that the Day of the Ghost has arrived, pulled it off in *Another Country.*

Of all black American novelists, and indeed of all American novelists of any hue, Richard Wright reigns supreme for his profound political, economic, and social reference. Wright had the ability, like Dreiser, of harnessing the gigantic, overwhelming environmental forces and focusing them, with pinpoint sharpness, on individuals and their acts as they are caught up in the whirlwind of the savage, anarchistic sweep of life, love, death, and hate, pain, hope, pleasure, and despair across the face of a nation and the world. But, ah! "O masters," it is Baldwin's work which is so void of a political, economic, or even a social reference. His characters all seem to be fucking and sucking in a vacuum. Baldwin has a superb touch when he speaks of human beings, when he is inside of them—especially his homosexuals—but he flounders when he looks beyond the skin; whereas Wright's forte, it seems to me, was in reflecting the intricate mechanisms of a social organization, its functioning as a unit.

Baldwin's essay on Richard Wright reveals that he despised—not Richard Wright, but his masculinity. He cannot confront the stud in others—except that he must either submit to it or destroy it. And he was not about to bow to a *black* man. Wright understood and lived the truth of what Norman Mailer meant when he said ". . . for being a man is the continuing battle of one's life, and one loses a bit of manhood with every stale compromise to the authority of any power in which one does not believe." Baldwin, compromised beyond getting back by the white man's *power,* which is real and which has nothing to do with *authority,* but to which Baldwin has ultimately succumbed psychologically, is totally unable to extricate himself from that horrible pain. It is the scourge of his art, because the only way out for him is psychologically to embrace Africa, the land of his fathers, which he utterly refuses to do. He has instead resorted to a despicable underground guerrilla war, waged on paper, against black masculinity, playing out the racial death-wish of Yacub, reaching, I think, a point where Mailer hits the spot: "Driven into defiance, it is natural if regrettable, that many homosexuals go to the direction of assuming that there is something intrinsically superior in homosexuality, and carried far enough it is a viewpoint which is as stultifying, as ridiculous, and as anti-human as the heterosexual's prejudice."

I, for one, do not think homosexuality is the latest advance over heterosexuality on the scale of human evolution. Homosexuality is a sickness, just as are baby-rape or wanting to become the head of General Motors.

A grave danger faces this nation, of which we are as yet unaware. And it is precisely this danger which Baldwin's work conceals; indeed, leads us away from. We are engaged in the deepest, the most fundamental revolution and reconstruction which men have ever been called upon to make in their lives, and which they absolutely cannot escape or avoid except at the peril of the very continued existence of human life on this planet. The time of the sham is over, and the cheek of the suffering saint must no longer be turned twice to the brute. The titillation of the guilt complexes of bored white liberals leads to doom. The grotesque hideousness of what is happening to us is reflected in this remark by Murray Kempton, quoted in *The Realist:* "When I was a boy Stepin Fetchit was the only Negro actor who worked regularly in the movies. . . . The fashion changes, but I sometimes think that Malcolm X and, to a degree even James Baldwin, are *our* Stepin Fetchits."

Yes, the fashion does change. "Will the machinegunners please step forward," said LeRoi Jones in a poem. "The machine gun on the corner," wrote Richard Wright, "is the symbol of the twentieth century." The embryonic spirit of kamikaze, real and alive, grows each day in the black man's heart and there are dreams of Nat Turner's legacy. The ghost of John Brown is creeping through suburbia. And I wonder if James Chaney said, as Andrew Goodman and Michael Schwerner stood helplessly watching, as the grizzly dogs crushed his bones with savage blows of chains—did poor James say, after Rufus Scott—*"You took the best, so why not take the rest?"* Or did he turn to his white brothers, seeing their plight, and say, after Baldwin, "That's your problem, baby!"

I say, after Mailer, "There's a shit-storm coming."

Rallying Round the Flag

I distinguished between two colonialisms, between a domestic one, and an external one. Capitalism at home is domestic colonialism.

—Osagyefo Kwame Nkrumah,
Consciencism.

Five years ago, even the most audacious visionary would not have dared predict the slashing do-or-die desperation and the sizzling up-tempo beat which has exploded into our politics, into our daily conversation, and into our nightmares and dreams. The ferment beneath the surface of our formal politics and public debate has grown more important in the last five years than at any time since the years preceding the Civil War. The parapolitics of the first Johnson Congress which, in contrast to most of its predecessors, seemed to resemble the dynamiting of a logjam, was actually sluggish, compromising, and drag-footish in terms of the pressing social problems which are feeding the conflagration raging in America's soul; problems which can no longer be compromised or swept cleverly under that national rug of self-delusion. The possibility of concealment no longer exists, and the only ones deceived are the deceivers themselves. Those who are victimized by these "social problems"—Negroes, the aged, unemployed and unemployable, the poor, the miseducated and dissatisfied students, the haters of war and lovers of man—have flung back the rug in outraged rebellion, refusing to be silenced until their grievances are uncompromisingly redressed. America has come alive deep down in its raw guts, and vast contending forces of revolutionary momentum are squaring off in this land for decisive showdowns from which no one can purchase sanctuary.

Americans are becoming increasingly polarized right and left, with the great body of the people in the middle confused and, sometimes to mask their confusion, feigning indifference. "Extremism of the right," "extremism of the left"—not since the '30s and the cringing McCarthy era have these slogans been armed with the power to kill. On the lips of articulate people today, "right" and "left" are verbal razor blades in a sense unparalleled in American history. California's former Governor Brown issued the ominous warning that "the stench of fascism is in the air." The last Republican presidential candidate was branded a right-wing extremist. And the FBI's J. Edgar Hoover, America's flattest foot, periodically issues grave reminders that left-wingers, having mastered deceit, are almost succeeding in subverting *this,* and are busily boring from within to take over *that.*

Both right and left claim to love their country. The Ku Klux Klan, John Birch Society, American Nazi Party, conservative Republicans, Minutemen, even the Hell's Angels —all wrap themselves up in the American flag and solemnly call themselves patriots. Their enemies and critics, seeing that the right wing would not disappear when spoofed as kooks, nuts, and little old ladies in tennis shoes, surprised and frightened by their potential strength as indicated by the 26,000,000 votes cast for Goldwater, now grant them *de facto* political status by applying to them such sophisticated labels as "neo-fascist" and "right-winger."

As for the left, all red-blooded Americans who love TV and gentle toilet tissue know that the Negro revolution was conceived in Moscow (scratch Moscow, insert Peking) and launched by left-wing fanatics, and that the growing mass movement in opposition to America's war in Vietnam is "Communist inspired, manipulated and controlled."

It is not an overstatement to say that the destiny of the entire human race depends on the outcome of what is going on in America today. This is a staggering reality to the rest of the world; they must feel like passengers in a supersonic jet liner who are forced to watch helplessly while a passle of drunks, hypes, freaks, and madmen fight for the controls and the pilot's seat. Whether America decisively moves to the right or to the left is the fundamental political problem in the world today; and the most serious question now before the American people is who now, in this post–civil rights era, are the true patriots, the new right or the new left?

The question of the Negro's place in America, which for a long time could actually be kicked around as a serious question, has been decisively resolved: he is here to stay. But the Negro revolution is the real bedrock of the battleground on which the new right and the new left are contending. In a sense, both the new left and the new right are the spawn of the Negro revolution. A broad national consensus was developed over the civil rights struggle, and it had the sophistication and morality to repudiate the right wing. This consensus, which stands between a violent nation and chaos, is America's most precious possession. But there are those who despise it.

The task which the new right has feverishly undertaken is to erode and break up this consensus, something that is a distinct possibility since the precise issues and conditions which gave birth to the consensus no longer exist.

On the other hand, the task of the new left has been to hold the consensus together during the period of transition from the civil rights struggle to the post–civil rights era, which may see the growth of a broader movement challenging the structure of political and economic power in America.

The fact that Johnson adopted Goldwater's foreign policy has severely disillusioned a significant sector of the consensus; many felt it was a betrayal of trust. This nation had just begun to relax after fighting a battle for its moral life, a battle which gave birth to a trust that became a holy cause; and the betrayal of this trust, this cause, may one day be looked upon as having laid the foundation of cynicism and political depravity that prepared the way for America's Hitler. Nevertheless, in seeking to hold the consensus together, the left is aided tremendously by the enemies it makes, and more so by the enemies it inherited from the civil rights struggle. The lewd spectacle of Dixicratic dinosaurs denouncing the protestants of the war in Vietnam can only infuriate and educate large sectors of the public who lost their bearings during the period of transition. All the new left need do is point: Look, there's old scurvy X, and dig who's with him—that filthy Y! Remember what they said about Selma?

At the same time, the link between America's undercover support of colonialism abroad and the bondage of the Negro at home becomes increasingly clearer. Those who are primarily concerned with improving the Negro's condition recognize, as do proponents of the liquidation of America's neo-colonial network, that their fight is one and the same. They see the key contradiction of our time.

We conceal something of the truth by saying that the new left merely opposes America's foreign policy. That is a euphemism for their support of national liberation in those areas of the world still under *de jure* colonial rule and those under the thumb of neo-colonial puppet regimes. The United States has the yes-or-no power of decision over all colonialism in the world today. There is not a colonial regime on the face of the earth today that could survive six months if the U.S. opposed it; and in many cases, without the active military and economic support of the U.S., the exploiting, murderous regimes would be dashed to bits by the exploited people themselves. The new left understands this thoroughly. It also knows that America's support of colonialism must be shattered before the resources and administrative machinery of the nation can be freed for the task of creating a truly free and humanistic society here at home. It is at this point, at the juncture of foreign policy and domestic policy, that the Negro revolution becomes one with the world revolution. Those who most bitterly oppose Negro progress are also the most ardent advocates of a belligerent foreign policy, the most violent castigators of critics of American escalation of war against the Vietnamese people, the hardest to die of the diehard enthusiasts of armed intervention in the internal affairs of the Dominican Republic and Latin America generally.

It is no coincidence that such political cavemen and fossilized intellects as Senator Stennis of Mississippi and Strom Thurmond of South Carolina were the first to speak out against the Vietnam Day demonstrations and protest marches held throughout America in October 1965. They who once spoke out so vehemently against the Negro revolution are still fighting the same war; they have merely retreated to different terrain. The massive upsurge of the Negro people and the support and sympathy aroused in the white community beat the dinosaurs back from their first line of defense: the color line. But these opponents of the Negro revolution, routed on the issue of civil rights, have by no means folded up their tents and slinked away disgracefully in defeat. They have regrouped and entrenched themselves on a new front. They understand that the Negro's basic situation cannot really change without structural changes in America's political and economic system.

What the Negro now needs and consciously seeks is political and economic power. And ultimately we shall witness the merging of the Negro revolution with a broader movement demanding disarmament and conversion of the economy to peaceful purposes. This prospect, of an alliance between the Negro revolution, the new left and the peace movement, fills the power structure with apprehension: witness the furious reaction provoked by Martin Luther King when he called for the cessation of American bombings of North Vietnam, negotiations with the National Liberation Front, and admission of China into the UN.

The fight against the Negro revolution, as long as this was possible, was waged in the name of the flag and the Constitution. Now, in this new stage of the struggle, the opposition is again employing as weapons the very same tools with which they have once been defeated. They are the only weapons remaining to the right-wing forces—short of naked terror and military repression to which they would eagerly resort if they saw no other way. Curiously, on this new level of struggle, they have much brighter hopes of success. The issues are more clouded. The moral issue has not yet become clear-cut as it was in the civil rights struggle. And the right is able to manipulate the people by playing upon the have-gun-will-travel streak in America's character, coupled with the narcissistic self-image as friend of the underdog. Americans think of themselves collectively as a huge rescue squad on twenty-four-hour call to any spot on the globe where dispute and conflict may erupt.

It does not make sense to the American people to fight a

war half-heartedly. Goldwater knew this when he campaigned for President, and the right knows it today. If America is at war in Vietnam, then it makes sense to Americans when the right wing indignantly demands the application of more and more force, increased bombings, gas, napalm, and even nuclear weapons, the use of any and all effective weapons to kill and defeat the enemy and get it over with. Americans like to get a job done, and what they hate most of all is to drag out a job when they have the means in their hands of completing it.

The Johnson administration feels obligated to obfuscate the issue by refusing to clarify to the American people the true nature of the Vietnam conflict. By interpreting the Vietnam situation as a war between two sovereign nations, the Communist North having invaded the peace-loving, democratic South, LBJ is able to pose as a courageous do-gooder coming to the aid of a weak underdog, while a cynical world, as usual, looks on and refuses to help Uncle Sam do his good deed. The power structure cannot publicly recognize that the Vietnamese conflict is a civil war, because such an acknowledgment would reveal us as an aggressor intervening on a favored side in a civil conflict. In fact, America's intervention has transformed a civil war into a war of national liberation.

The President cannot afford to tell the truth to the American people because he knows they would not support the war if they really understood. It is only by keeping them confused and hysterical—the job of the vast, centralized, collusive mass media—that LBJ is able to get away with it. And this is the source of Johnson's great fear of the teach-ins and protest demonstrations. The truth is electric and it spreads, spreads, spreads. What galls Johnson and the new right is the fear that the mounting protests against their policy will awaken the American people. They know that masses of Americans would come out to demonstrate against LBJ. Mass embarrassment—at such obviously hypocritical actions as the American intervention in the Dominican Republic on the bloody side of a right-wing military *junta*—might turn to mass anger.

The world capitalist system has come to a decisive fork in the road, and this is at the heart of our national crisis. The road to the left is the way of reconciliation with the exploited people of the world, the liberation of all peoples, the dismantling of all economic relations based upon the exploitation of man by man, universal disarmament, and the establishment of international rule of law with effective means of enforcement. The road to the right is refusal to submit to the universal demand for national liberation, economic justice, peace, and popular sovereignty. To walk this last path, the decision-makers must be prepared to unleash worldwide genocide, including the extermination of America's Negroes. The people within these countries who try to stand against the will of the overwhelming majority of the human race must be willing to forgo the last traces of their own liberty and see their governments turned into totalitarian regimes tolerating no dissent. The rage of the American power structure over the exercise of the constitutional right to dissent, to assemble and peacefully petition against Johnson's war in Vietnam, is only a mild taste of the hemlock the people will be forced to swallow if they allow their country to go down the death-seeking branch of the fork.

President Kennedy gave the distinct impression of commitment to the path of reconciliation, and it was the source of much of his appeal. What frightens people about President Johnson is that he seems to be trying to walk down both roads simultaneously. But he cannot play his double game for long. Sooner or later he and his successors will have to choose.

The new right and the new left in America, each trying to lead the nation down the diverging branches of the fork, have between them the fate of the world and the hopes of a tortured, bleeding humanity—forever seeking life and almost always receiving betrayal and death from the outstretched hand of the seducer.

The Black Man's Stake
in Vietnam

The most critical tests facing Johnson are the war in Vietnam and the Negro revolution at home. The fact that the brains in the Pentagon see fit to send 16 per cent black troops to Vietnam is one indication that there is a structural relationship between these two arenas of conflict. And the initial outrageous refusal of the Georgia Legislature to seat representative-elect Julian Bond, because he denounced the aggressive U.S. role in Vietnam, shows, too, the very intimate relationship between the way human beings are being treated in Vietnam and the treatment they are receiving here in the United States.

We live today in a system that is in the last stages of the protracted process of breaking up on a worldwide basis. The rulers of this system have their hands full. Injustice is being challenged at every turn and on every level. The rulers perceive the greatest threat to be the national liberation movements around the world, particularly in Asia, Africa, and Latin America. In order for them to wage wars of suppression against these national liberation movements abroad, they must have peace and stability and unanimity of purpose at home. But at home there is a Trojan Horse, a Black Trojan Horse that has become aware of itself and is

now struggling to get on its feet. It, too, demands liberation.

What is the purpose of the attention that the rulers are
now focusing on the Trojan Horse? Is it out of a newfound
love for the horse, or is it because the rulers need the horse
to be quiet, to be still, and not cause the rulers, already with
their backs pressed to the wall, any trouble or embarrassment while they force the war in Vietnam? Indeed, the
rulers have need of the horse's power on the fields of battle.
What the black man in America must keep constantly in
mind is that the doctrine of white supremacy, which is a
part of the ideology of the world system the power structure
is trying to preserve, lets the black man in for the greatest
portion of the suffering and hate which white supremacy
has dished out to the non-white people of the world for
hundreds of years. The white-supremacy-oriented white
man feels less compunction about massacring "niggers"
than he does about massacring any other race of people on
earth. This historically indisputable fact, taken with the
present persistent efforts of the United States to woo the
Soviet Union into an alliance against China, spells *DAN-
GER* to all the peoples of the world who have been victims
of white supremacy. If this sweethearting proves successful,
if the United States is finally able to make a match with
Russia, or if the U.S. can continue to frighten the Soviet
Union into reneging on its commitments to international
socialist solidarity (about which the Soviets are always
trumpeting, while still allowing the imperialist aggressors to
daily bomb the Democratic Republic of North Vietnam),
and if the U.S. is able to unleash its anxious fury and armed
might against the rising non-white giant of China, which is
the real target of U.S. policy in Vietnam and the Object-
Evil of U.S. strategy the world over—if the U.S. is successful in these areas, then it will be the black man's turn

again to face the lyncher and burner of the world: and face him alone.

Black Americans are too easily deceived by a few smiles and friendly gestures, by the passing of a few liberal-sounding laws which are left on the books to rot unenforced, and by the mushy speechmaking of a President who is a past master of talking out of the thousand sides of his mouth. Such poetry does not *guarantee* the safe future of the black people in America. The black people must have a guarantee, they must be *certain,* they must be sure beyond all doubt that the reign of terror is ended and not just suspended, and that the future of their people is secure. And the only way they can ensure this is to gain organizational unity and communication with their brothers and allies around the world, on an international basis. They must have this power. There is no other way. Anything else is a sellout of the future of their people. The world of today was fashioned yesterday. What is involved here, what is being decided right now, is the shape of power in the world tomorrow.

The American racial problem can no longer be spoken of or solved in isolation. The relationship between the genocide in Vietnam and the smiles of the white man toward black Americans is a direct relationship. Once the white man solves his problem in the East he will then turn his fury again on the black people of America, his longtime punching bag. The black people have been tricked again and again, sold out at every turn by *mis*leaders. After the Civil War, America went through a period similar to the one we are now in. The Negro problem received a full hearing. Everybody knew that the black man had been denied justice. No one doubted that it was time for changes and that the black man should be made a first-class citizen. But Reconstruction ended. Blacks who had been elevated to high positions were brusquely kicked out into the streets and herded along with the masses of blacks into the ghettos and black belts. The lyncher and the burner received virtual license to murder blacks at will. White Americans found a new level on which to cool the blacks out. And with the help of such tools as Booker T. Washington, the doctrine of segregation was clamped firmly onto the backs of the blacks. It has taken a hundred years to struggle up from that level of cool-out to the miserable position that black Americans now find themselves in. Time is passing. The historical opportunity which world events now present to black Americans is running out with every tick of the clock.

This is the last act of the show. We are living in a time when the people of the world are making their final bid for full and complete freedom. Never before in history has this condition prevailed. Always before there have been more or less articulate and aware pockets of people, portions of classes, etc., but today's is an era of mass awareness, when the smallest man on the street is in rebellion against the system which has denied him life and which he has come to understand robs him of his dignity and self-respect. Yet he is being told that it will take time to get programs started, to pass legislation, to educate white people into accepting the idea that black people want and deserve freedom. But it is physically impossible to move as fast as the black man would like to move. Black men are deadly serious when they say *FREEDOM NOW*. Even if the white man wanted to eradicate all traces of evil overnight, he would not be able to do it because the economic and political system will not permit it. All talk about going too fast is treasonous to the black man's future.

What the white man must be brought to understand is that the black man in America today is fully aware of his position, and he does not intend to be tricked again into another hundred-year forfeit of freedom. Not for a single moment or for any price will the black men now rising up in America settle for anything less than their full proportionate share and participation in the sovereignty of America. The black man has already come to a realization that to be free it is necessary for him to throw his life—everything—on the line, because the oppressors refuse to understand that it is now impossible for them to come up with another trick to squelch the black revolution. The black man can't afford to take a chance. He can't afford to put things off. He must stop the whole show *NOW* and get his business straight, because if he does not do it now, if he fails to grasp securely the reins of this historic opportunity, there may be no tomorrow for him.

The black man's interest lies in seeing a free and independent Vietnam, a strong Vietnam which is not the puppet of international white supremacy. If the nations of Asia, Latin America, and Africa are strong and free, the black man in America will be safe and secure and free to live in dignity and self-respect. It is a cold fact that while the nations of Africa, Asia, and Latin America were shackled in colonial bondage, the black American was held tightly in the vise of oppression and not permitted to utter a sound of protest of any effect. But when these nations started bidding for their freedom, it was then that black Americans were able to seize the chance; it was then that the white man yielded what little he did—out of sheer necessity. The only lasting salvation for the black American is to do all he can to see to it that the African, Asian, and Latin American nations are free and independent.

In this regard, black Americans have a big role to play. They are a Black Trojan Horse within white America and they number in excess of 23,000,000 strong. That is a lot of strength. But it is a lot of weakness if it is disorganized and at odds with itself. Right now it is deplorably disorganized, and the overriding need is for unity and organization. Unity is on all black lips. Today we stand on the verge of sweeping change in this wretched landscape of a thousand little fragmented and ineffectual groups and organizations unable to work together for the common cause. *The need for one organization that will give one voice to the black man's common interest* is felt in every bone and fiber of black America.

Yesterday, after firmly repudiating racism and breaking his ties with the Black Muslim organization, the late Malcolm X launched a campaign to transform the American black man's struggle from the narrow plea for "civil rights" to the universal demand for human rights, with the ultimate aim of bringing the United States government to task before the United Nations. This, and the idea of the Organization of Afro-American Unity, was Malcolm's dying legacy to his people. It did not fall on barren ground. Already, black American leaders have met with the ambassadors of black Africa at a luncheon at UN headquarters. The meaning of this momentous event is lost on no one. The fact that it was the issue of Julian Bond, his denunciation of U.S. aggression in Vietnam, and the action of racist elements in the Georgia legislature which brought the leaders of black Africa and black America together is prophetic of an even clearer recognition by black men that their interests are also threatened by the U.S. war of suppression in Vietnam. This dovetailing of causes and issues is destined to bring to fruition the other dream which Malcolm's assassination prevented him from realizing—the Organization of Afro-American Unity, or perhaps a similar organization under a different name. Black Americans now realize that they must organize for the power to change the foreign and domestic policies of the U.S. government. They must let their voice be heard on these issues. They must let the world know where they stand.

It is no accident that the U.S. government is sending all those black troops to Vietnam. Some people think that America's point in sending 16 per cent black troops to Vietnam is to kill off the cream of black youth. But it has another important result. By turning her black troops into butchers of the Vietnamese people, America is spreading hate against the black race throughout Asia. Even black Africans find it hard not to hate black Americans for being so stupid as to allow themselves to be used to slaughter another people who are fighting to be free. Black Americans are considered to be the world's biggest fools to go to another country to fight for something they don't have for themselves.

It bothers white racists that people around the world love black Americans but find it impossible to give a similar warm affection to white Americans. The white racist knows that he is the Ugly American and he wants the black American to be Ugly, too, in the eyes of the world: misery loves company! When the people around the world cry "Yankee, Go Home!" they mean the white man, not the black man who is a recently freed slave. The white man is deliberately trying to make the people of the world turn against black Americans, because he knows that the day is coming when black Americans will need the help and support of their brothers, friends, and natural allies around the world. If through stupidity or by following hand-picked leaders who are the servile agents of the power structure, black Americans allow this strategy to succeed against them, then when the time comes and they need this help and support from around the world, it will not be there. All of the international love, respect, and goodwill that black Americans now have around the world will have dried up. They themselves will have buried it in the mud of the rice paddies of Vietnam.

Domestic Law
and International Order

The police department and the armed forces are the two arms of the power structure, the muscles of control and enforcement. They have deadly weapons with which to inflict pain on the human body. They know how to bring about horrible deaths. They have clubs with which to beat the body and the head. They have bullets and guns with which to tear holes in the flesh, to smash bones, to disable and kill. They use force, to make you do what the deciders have decided you must do.

Every country on earth has these agencies of force. The people everywhere fear this terror and force. To them it is like a snarling wild beast which can put an end to one's dreams. They punish. They have cells and prisons to lock you up in. They pass out sentences. They won't let you go when you want to. You have to stay put until they give the word. If your mother is dying, you can't go to her bedside to say goodbye or to her graveside to see her lowered into the earth, to see her, for the last time, swallowed up by that black hole.

The techniques of the enforcers are many: firing squads, gas chambers, electric chairs, torture chambers, the garrote, the guillotine, the tightening rope around your throat. It has been found that the death penalty is necessary to back up the law, to make it easier to enforce, to deter transgressions against the penal code. That everybody doesn't believe in the same laws is beside the point.

Which laws get enforced depends on who is in power. If the capitalists are in power, they enforce laws designed to protect their system, their way of life. They have a particular abhorrence for crimes against property, but are prepared to be liberal and show a modicum of compassion for crimes against the person—unless, of course, an instance of the latter is combined with an instance of the former. In such cases, nothing can stop them from throwing the whole book at the offender. For instance, armed robbery with violence, to a capitalist, is the very epitome of evil. Ask any banker what he thinks of it.

If Communists are in power, they enforce laws designed to protect their system, their way of life. To them, the horror of horrors is the speculator, that man of magic who has mastered the art of getting something with nothing and who in America would be a member in good standing of his local Chamber of Commerce.

"The people," however, are nowhere consulted, although everywhere everything is done always in their name and ostensibly for their betterment, while their real-life problems go unsolved. "The people" are a rubber stamp for the crafty and sly. And no problem can be solved without taking the police department and the armed forces into account. Both kings and bookies understand this, as do first ladies and common prostitutes.

The police do on the domestic level what the armed forces do on the international level: protect the way of life of those in power. The police patrol the city, cordon off communities, blockade neighborhoods, invade homes, search for that which is hidden. The armed forces patrol the world, invade countries and continents, cordon off nations, blockade islands and whole peoples; they will also overrun villages, neighborhoods, enter homes, huts, caves, searching for that which is hidden. The policeman and the soldier will violate your person, smoke you out with various gases. Each will shoot you, beat your head and body with sticks and clubs, with rifle butts, run you through with bayonets, shoot holes in your flesh, kill you. They each have unlimited firepower. They will use all that is necessary to bring you to your knees. They won't take no for an answer. If you resist their sticks, they draw their guns. If you resist their guns, they call for reinforcements with bigger guns. Eventually they will come in tanks, in jets, in ships. They will not rest until you surrender or are killed. The policeman and the soldier will have the last word.

Both police and the armed forces follow orders. Orders. Orders flow from the top down. Up there, behind closed doors, in antechambers, in conference rooms, gavels bang on the tables, the tinkling of silver decanters can be heard as icewater is poured by well-fed, conservatively dressed men in hornrimmed glasses, fashionably dressed American widows with rejuvenated faces and tinted hair, the air permeated with the square humor of Bob Hope jokes. Here all the talking is done, all the thinking, all the deciding. Gray rabbits of men scurry forth from the conference room to spread the decisions throughout the city, as News. Carrying out orders is a job, a way of meeting the payments on the house, a way of providing for one's kiddies. In the armed forces it is also a duty, patriotism. Not to do so is treason.

Every city has its police department. No city would be complete without one. It would be sheer madness to try operating an American city without the heat, the fuzz, the man. Americans are too far gone, or else they haven't arrived yet; the center does not exist, only the extremes.

Take away the cops and Americans would have a coast-to-coast free-for-all. There are, of course, a few citizens who carry their own private cops around with them, built into their souls. But there is robbery in the land, and larceny, murder, rape, burglary, theft, swindles, all brands of crime, profit, rent, interest—and these blasé descendants of Pilgrims are at each other's throats. To complicate matters, there are also rich people and poor people in America. There are Negroes and whites, Indians, Puerto Ricans, Mexicans, Jews, Chinese, Arabs, Japanese—all with equal rights but unequal possessions. Some are haves and some are have-nots. All have been taught to worship at the shrine of General Motors. The whites are on top in America and they want to stay there, up there. They are also on top in the world, on the international level, and they want to stay up there, too. Everywhere there are those who want to smash this precious toy clock of a system, they want ever so much to change it, to rearrange things, to pull the whites down off their high horse and make them equal. Everywhere the whites are fighting to prolong their status, to retard the erosion of their position. In America, when everything else fails, they call out the police. On the international level, when everything else fails, they call out the armed forces.

A strange thing happened in Watts, in 1965, August. The blacks, who in this land of private property have all private and no property, got excited into an uproar because they noticed a cop before he had a chance to wash the blood off his hands. Usually the police department can handle such flare-ups. But this time it was different. Things got out of hand. The blacks were running amok, burning, shooting, breaking. The police department was powerless to control them; the chief called for reinforcements. Out came the National Guard, that ambiguous hybrid from the twilight zone where the domestic army merges with the international; that hypocritical force poised within America and capable of action on either level, capable of backing up either the police or the armed forces. Unleashing their formidable firepower, they crushed the blacks. But things will never be the same again. Too many people saw that those who turned the other cheek in Watts got their whole head blown off. At the same time, heads were being blown off in Vietnam. America was embarrassed, not by the quality of her deeds but by the surplus of publicity focused upon her negative selling points, and a little frightened because of what all those dead bodies, on two fronts, implied. Those corpses spoke eloquently of potential allies and alliances. A community of interest began to emerge, dripping with blood, out of the ashes of Watts. The blacks in Watts and all over America could now see the Viet Cong's point: both were on the receiving end of what the armed forces were dishing out.

So now the blacks, stung by the new knowledge they have unearthed, cry out: *"POLICE BRUTALITY!"* From one end of the country to the other, the new war cry is raised. The youth, those nodes of compulsive energy who are all fuel and muscle, race their motors, itch to do something. The Uncle Toms, no longer willing to get down on their knees to lick boots, do so from a squatting position. The black bourgeoisie call for Citizens' Review Boards, to assert civilian control over the activity of the police. In back rooms, in dark stinking corners of the ghettos, self-conscious black men curse their own cowardice and stare at their rifles and pistols and shotguns laid out on tables before them, trembling as they wish for a manly impulse to course through their bodies and send them screaming mad into the streets shooting from the hip. Black women look at their men as if they are bugs, curious growths of flesh playing an inscrutable waiting game. Violence becomes a homing pigeon floating through the ghettos seeking a black brain in which to roost for a season.

In their rage against the police, against police brutality, the blacks lose sight of the fundamental reality: that the police are only an instrument for the implementation of the policies of those who make the decisions. Police brutality is only one facet of the crystal of terror and oppression. Behind police brutality there is social brutality, economic brutality, and political brutality. From the perspective of the ghetto, this is not easy to discern: the TV newscaster and the radio announcer and the editorialists of the newspapers are wizards of the smoke screen and the snow job.

What is true on the international level is true also at home; except that the ace up the sleeve is easier to detect in the international arena. Who would maintain that American soldiers are in Vietnam on their own motion? They were conscripted into the armed forces and taught the wisdom of obeying orders. They were sent to Vietnam by orders of the generals in the Pentagon, who receive them from the Secretary of Defense, who receives them from the President, who is shrouded in mystery. The soldier in the field in Vietnam, the man who lies in the grass and squeezes the trigger when a little half-starved, trembling Vietnamese peasant crosses his sights, is only following orders, carrying out a policy and a plan. He hardly knows what it is all about. They have him wired-up tight with the slogans of TV and the World Series. All he knows is that he has been assigned to carry out a certain ritual of duties. He is well trained and does the best he can. He does a good job. He may want to please those above him with the quality of his performance. He may want to make sergeant, or better. This man is from some hicky farm in Shit Creek, Georgia.

He only knew whom to kill after passing through boot camp. He could just as well come out ready to kill Swedes. He will kill a Swede dead, if he is ordered to do so.

Same for the policeman in Watts. He is not there on his own. They have all been assigned. They have been told what to do and what not to do. They have also been told what they better not do. So when they continually do something, in every filthy ghetto in this shitty land, it means only that they are following orders.

It's no secret that in America the blacks are in total rebellion against the System. They want to get their nuts out of the sand. They don't like the way America is run, from top to bottom. In America, everything is owned. Everything is held as private property. Someone has a brand on everything. There is nothing left over. Until recently, the blacks themselves were counted as part of somebody's private property, along with the chickens and goats. The blacks have not forgotten this, principally because they are still treated as if they are part of someone's inventory of assets—or perhaps, in this day of rage against the costs of welfare, blacks are listed among the nation's liabilities. On any account, however, blacks are in no position to respect or help maintain the institution of private property. What they want is to figure out a way to get some of that property for themselves, to divert it to their own needs. This is what it is all about, and this is the real brutality involved. This is the source of all brutality.

The police are the armed guardians of the social order. The blacks are the chief domestic victims of the American social order. A conflict of interest exists, therefore, between the blacks and the police. It is not solely a matter of trigger-happy cops, of brutal cops who love to crack black heads. Mostly it's a job to them. It pays good. And there are numerous fringe benefits. The real problem is a trigger-happy social order.

The Utopians speak of a day when there will be no police. There will be nothing for them to do. Every man will do his duty, will respect the rights of his neighbor, will not disturb the peace. The needs of all will be taken care of. Everyone will have sympathy for his fellow man. There will be no such thing as crime. There will be, of course, no prisons. No electric chairs, no gas chambers. The hangman's rope will be the thing of the past. The entire earth will be a land of plenty. There will be no crimes against property, no speculation.

It is easy to see that we are not on the verge of entering Utopia: there are cops everywhere. North and South, the Negroes are the have-nots. They see property all around them, property that is owned by whites. In this regard, the black bourgeoisie has become nothing but a ridiculous nuisance. Having waged a battle for entrance into the American mainstream continually for fifty years, all of the black bourgeoisie's defenses are directed outward, against the whites. They have no defenses against the blacks and no time to erect any. The black masses can handle them any time they choose, with one mighty blow. But the white bourgeoisie presents a bigger problem, those whites who own everything. With many shackled by unemployment, hatred in black hearts for this system of private property increases daily. The sanctity surrounding property is being called into question. The mystique of the deed of ownership is melting away. In other parts of the world, peasants rise up and expropriate the land from the former owners. Blacks in America see that the deed is not eternal, that it is not signed by God, and that new deeds, making blacks the owners, can be drawn up.

The Black Muslims raised the cry, *"WE MUST HAVE SOME LAND!" "SOME LAND OF OUR OWN OR ELSE!"* Blacks in America shrink from the colossus of General Motors. They can't see how to wade through that thicket of common stocks, preferred stocks, bonds and debentures. They only know that General Motors is huge, that it has billions of dollars under its control, that it owns land, that its subsidiaries are legion, that it is a repository of vast powers. The blacks want to crack the nut of General Motors. They are meditating on it. Meanwhile, they must learn that the police take orders from General Motors. And that the Bank of America has something to do with them even though they don't have a righteous penny in the bank. They have no bank accounts, only bills to pay. The only way they know of making withdrawals from the bank is at the point of a gun. The shiny fronts of skyscrapers intimidate them. They do not own them. They feel alienated from the very sidewalks on which they walk. This white man's country, this white man's world. Overflowing with men of color. An economy consecrated to the succor of the whites. Blacks are incidental. The war on poverty, that monstrous insult to the rippling muscles in a black man's arms, is an index of how men actually sit down and plot each other's deaths, actually sit down with slide rules and calculate how to hide bread from the hungry. And the black bourgeoisie greedily sopping up what crumbs are tossed into their dark corner.

There are 20,000,000 of these blacks in America, probably more. Today they repeat, in awe, this magic number to themselves: there are 20,000,000 of us! They shout this to each other in humiliated astonishment. No one need tell them that there is vast power latent in their mass. They know that 20,000,000 of anything is enough to get some recognition and consideration. They know also that they must harness their number and hone it into a sword with a sharp cutting edge. White General Motors also knows that the unity of these 20,000,000 ragamuffins will spell the death of the system of its being. At all costs, then, they will seek to keep these blacks from uniting, from becoming bold and revolutionary. These white property owners know that they must keep the blacks cowardly and intimidated. By a complex communications system of hints and signals, certain orders are given to the chief of police and the sheriff, who pass them on to their men, the footsoldiers in the trenches of the ghetto.

We experience this system of control as madness. So that Leonard Deadwyler, one of these 20,000,000 blacks, is rushing his pregnant wife to the hospital and is shot dead by a policeman. An accident. That the sun rises in the east and sets in the west is also an accident, by design. The blacks are up in arms. From one end of America to the other, blacks are outraged at this accident, this latest evidence of what an accident-prone people they are, of the cruelty and pain of their lives, these blacks at the mercy of trigger-happy Yankees and Rebs in coalition against their skin. They want the policeman's blood as a sign that the Viet Cong is not the only answer. A sign to save them from the deaths they must die, and inflict. The power structure, without so much as blinking an eye, wouldn't mind tossing Bova to the mob, to restore law and order, but it knows in the vaults of its strength that at all cost the blacks must be kept at bay, that it must uphold the police department, its Guardian. Nothing must be allowed to threaten the set-up. Justice is secondary. Security is the byword.

Meanwhile, blacks are looking on and asking tactical questions. They are asked to die for the System in Vietnam. In Watts they are killed by it. Now—*NOW!*—they are asking each other, in dead earnest: Why not die right here in Babylon fighting for a better life, like the Viet Cong? If those little cats can do it, what's wrong with big studs like us?

A mood sets in, spreads across America, across the face of Babylon, jells in black hearts everywhere.

III: Prelude to Love
—Three Letters

[*Note:* Eldridge Cleaver had been in prison in California for nearly nine years. Beverly Axelrod is a San Francisco lawyer. Prior to the time the following letters were written, Mr. Cleaver had written to Mrs. Axelrod for legal assistance. She had visited him three times before the following exchange of letters took place.]

Eldridge Cleaver
Folsom Prison
Represa, California
September 5, 1965

Dear Beverly Axelrod:

For two charged days and restless nights after you left, I loafed in the case of my skull, feeling prematurely embalmed in some magical ethered mist dispensed by the dialectic of our contact. When I left you sitting in that little glass cage, which I must somehow learn to respect because it has a special, eternal meaning now, I did not stop or pause. Including the door to that glass cage, and counting the door of my cell, I passed through twelve assorted gates

and doors before collapsing on my narrow bed, staggering
under the weight of the DAY. The doors and gates swung
open before me as I advanced upon them, as I charged
down on them, as if they were activated by photoelectric
cells responding to my approach. I walked swiftly, but I felt
myself to be running, stumbling, thrashing and flailing with
my arms to clear a passage through dense, tangled vines. I
spoke to no one, recognized no one, and I felt that no one
could see or recognize me (wrong: I was accused next day
of walking past a couple of henchmen as if they weren't
even there. I kept telling them that, in fact, as far as I was
concerned, they weren't there, but they refuse to believe in
their own non-existence or invisibility).

On the third day I arose again from the damned. No,
that's going too far!

What a transfusion! I don't believe I can stand you in
such massive doses. It may prove lethal.

I am almost afraid to return to my manuscripts—which
themselves seem to cringe from me—after talking with you.
I know I shall remain immobile, transfixed, until I've gotten
this letter off to you. Then. . . .

I really have no sense of myself and I have always
suffered under the compliments of others, especially my
friends. I panic. I ran for an office in the Folsom Gavel
Club recently. One of my boosters poured lavish praise
upon me and my qualifications for the job. I squirmed in
my seat and felt oppressed. Does this mean that I do not
have the ego for a compliment? No, it does not. It's hypocritical of me, but whenever someone says something nice
about me, it sort of knocks me for a loop. And you? The
things you said sent me spinning. But don't stop, let me
suffer—and overcome.

I feel impelled to express myself to you extravagantly,

and words, phrases, sentences, paragraphs leap in my mind.
But I beat them down, refuse to write them, because it all
seems so predictable and trite. I feel humiliated by the
words you inspire me to write to you. I refuse to write them.
What right have you to summon my soul from its slumber?
But it's all golden and I write this from a sense of the
sweetness of irony, the better to marvel at the unbelievable
sequence of chance events which brought us face to face in
a little glass cage in the office of the Warden of Folsom
Prison.

You have tossed me a lifeline. If you only knew how I'd
been drowning, how I'd considered that I'd gone down for
the third time long ago, how I kept thrashing around in the
water simply because I still felt the impulse to fight back
and the tug of a distant shore, how I sat in a rage that night
with the polysyllabic burden of your name pounding in my
brain—Beverly Axelrod, Beverly Axelrod—and out of
what instinct did I decide to write to you? It was a gamble
on an equation constructed in delirium, and it was right.

Let me say this. I was 22 when I came to prison and of
course I have changed tremendously over the years. But I
had always had a strong sense of myself and in the last few
years I felt I was losing my identity. There was a deadness
in my body that eluded me, as though I could not exactly
locate its site. I would be aware of this numbness, this
feeling of atrophy, and it haunted the back of my mind.
Because of this numb spot, I felt peculiarly off balance, the
awareness of something missing, of a blank spot, a certain
intimation of emptiness. Now I know what it was. And
since encountering you, I feel life strength flowing back into
that spot. My step, the tread of my stride, which was becoming tentative and uncertain, has begun to recover and
take on a new definiteness, a confidence, a boldness which

makes me want to kick over a few tables. I may even swagger a little, and, as I read in a book somewhere, "push myself forward like a train."

NOW TURN THE RECORD OVER AND PLAY THE OTHER SIDE

I have tried to mislead you. I am not humble at all. I have no humility and I do not fear you in the least. If I pretend to be shy, if I appear to hesitate, it is only a sham to deceive. By playing the humble part, I sucker my fellow men in and seduce them of their trust. And then, if it suits my advantage, I lower the boom—mercilessly. I lied when I stated that I had no sense of myself. I am very well aware of my style. My vanity is as vast as the scope of a dream, my heart is that of a tyrant, my arm is the arm of the Executioner. It is only the failure of my plots that I fear. Whereas in the past we have had Prophets of Doom, in my vanity I wish to be the Voice of Doom itself. I am angry at the insurgents of Watts. They have pulled the covers off me and revealed to all what potential may lie behind my Tom Smile. I had planned to run for President of the United States. My slogan?

PUT A BLACK FINGER ON THE NUCLEAR TRIGGER.

400 years of docility, of being calm, cool and collected under stress and strain would go to prove that I was the man for the job, that I would not panic in a crisis and push the button. I could be counted on to be cool. It was a cinch, I had it made—but then came Watts! All my plans went up in smoke! And so, with worn-out tools, I stoop to begin again.

Please take care of yourself.

Until something happens, I shall remain, because I have no other choice—and even if I had another choice I would still remain—

Most Emphatically Yours,
Eldridge

Beverly Axelrod
Attorney-at-Law
San Francisco, Calif.
September 10, 1965

Dear Eldridge Cleaver:

. . . The need for expression is now upon me, having finished the legal matters, and I'm getting panicky. I'm not strong enough to take the safest course, which would be to not widen the subject matter of our correspondence, and I'm having a terrible time trying to say what I want knowing it will be read by the censors.

Your letter, which I keep rereading, shows you're going through the same turmoil I am; but I bear the onus of having allowed it. You talk about it being lethal, and then about life coming back—and I know that both are true.

I'm going purely on instinct now, which is not usual for me, but somehow I know I'm right, or maybe it's just that it's so important that I don't care about the risk of being wrong. Am I coming through to you? I'm writing I know in an obscure kind of way because of the damnable lack of privacy in our communications.

Believe this: I accept you. I know you little and I know you much, but whichever way it goes, I accept you. Your manhood comes through in a thousand ways, rare and wonderful. I'm out in the world, with an infinity of choices. You don't have to wonder if I'm grasping at something because I have no real measuring stick. I accept you.

About that other side of the record: Did you really think I didn't know? Another facet of the crystal might be an apter term; I have a few facets myself. I do not fear you, I know you will not hurt me. Your hatred is large, but not nearly so vast as you sometimes imagine; it can be used, but it can also be soothed and softened.

What an enormous amount of exploring we have to do! I feel as though I'm on the edge of a new world.

Memo to me: Be rational. It cannot be resolved. The choices: 1. He believes everything he says, but he cannot know, he has no choice; or 2. It's a beautiful put-on because he doesn't know that you would do exactly what you are doing for him anyway; or 3. It's a game to relieve the monotony, conscious or not. Answer: It doesn't make a damn bit of difference, because I can't find out, he can't find out, and it's too late anyway. The only important thing is to get him out, and that was obvious from the first letter, with all lawyerlike objectivity.

What an awesome thing it is to feel oneself on the verge of the possibility of really knowing another person. Can it ever happen? I'm not sure. I don't know that any two people can really strip themselves that naked in front of each other. We're so filled with fears of rejection and pretenses that we scarcely know whether we're being fraudulent or real ourselves.

Of all the dangers we share, probably the greatest comes from our fantasizing about each other. Are we making each other up? We have no way of testing the reality of it.

I can't write any more. I'm thunderstruck at having written this much. I'm afraid to read it over, because it's likely I would tear it up, so I'll send it as is. Can you imagine how much I haven't said?

Sincerely yours,
Beverly Axelrod

Eldridge Cleaver
Folsom Prison
Represa, California
September 15, 1965

Dear Beverly Axelrod:

Your letters to me are living pieces—chunks!—of you, and are the most important things in my life. This is fantastic. It only happens in books—or in the dreams of inmates of insane asylums—and with people who are for real. I share with you the awesome feeling of being on the verge of really knowing another person.

I place a great deal of emphasis on people really listening to each other, to what the person has to say, because one seldom encounters a person capable of taking either you or themselves seriously. But I was not *really* like this when I was out of prison—although the seeds were there, but there was too much confusion and madness mixed in. I was not too interested in communicating with other people—that is not true. What I mean is, I had a profound desire for communicating with and getting to know other people, but I was incapable of doing so, I didn't know how.

Do you know what shameless thought just bullied its way into my consciousness? That I deserve you, that I deserve to know you and to communicate with you, that I deserve to have all this happening. What have I done to merit this? I don't believe in the merit system. I Am That I Am. No, I will not hurt you.

Memo to us: 1. He believes everything he says and knows what he is saying; 2. Put-ons are cruel, and how could I be cruel to you? 3. He does not play games, and he does not find life monotonous, conscious or not. He has plans and

dreams, and he is deadly serious. Answer: It makes every
bit of difference, and I hope to help you find out, he is already finding out; taking it like you find it is a burn, it sells
yourself short: be discerning and take only after you spot
what you like—but I'm hoping that it is too late for you to
flip over on me because it is certainly much too late for
me.

Your thought, "Of all the dangers we share, probably the
greatest comes from our fantasizing about each other. Are
we making each other up?" bothers me. It would be very
simple if that were the case: I could arrange (and how easy
it would be!) to spend the rest of my life in prison and we
could live happily ever after. But it is not that easy, is it? I
seek a lasting relationship, something permanent in a world
of change, in which all is transitory, ephemeral, and full of
pain. We humans, we are too frail creatures to handle such
titanic emotions and deep magnetic yearnings, strivings and
impulses.

The reason two people are reluctant to really strip
themselves naked in front of each other is because in doing
so they make themselves vulnerable and give enormous
power over themselves one to the other. How awful, how
deadly, how catastrophically they can hurt each other,
wreck and ruin each other forever! How often, indeed, they
end by inflicting pain and torment upon each other. Better
to maintain shallow, superficial affairs; that way the scars
are not too deep, no blood is hacked from the soul. You
beautifully—O, how beautifully!!—spoke, in your letter, of
"What an awesome thing it is to feel oneself on the verge of
the possibility of really knowing another person . . ." and
"I feel as though I am on the edge of a new world." Getting
to know someone, entering that new world, is an ultimate,
irretrievable leap into the unknown. The prospect is terrifying. The stakes are high. The emotions are overwhelming.

In human experience, only the perennial themes can move us to such an extent. Death. Birth. The Grave. Love. Hate.

I do not believe that a beautiful relationship has to always end in carnage. I do not believe that we have to be fraudulent and pretentious, because that is the source of future difficulties and ultimate failure. If we project fraudulent, pretentious images, or if we fantasize each other into distorted caricatures of what we really are, then, when we awake from the trance and see beyond the sham and front, all will dissolve, all will die and transform into bitterness and hate. I know that sometimes people fake on each other out of genuine motives to hold onto the object of their tenderest feelings. They see themselves as so inadequate that they feel forced to wear a mask in order to continuously impress the other. I do not want to "hold" you, I want you to "stay" out of your own need for me.

I seek the profound. Contrary to the advice of the Prophet, I'll take the credit and let the cash go. What I feel for you is profound. Beverly, there is something happening between us that is way out of the ordinary. Ours is one for the books, for the poets to draw new inspiration from, one to silence the cynics, and one to humble us by reminding us of how little we know about human beings, about ourselves. I did not know that I had all these feelings inside me. They have never been aroused before. Now they cascade down upon my head and threaten to beat me down to the ground, into the dust. But because of the strength of the magnetic pull I feel toward you, I am not fazed and I know that I can stand against the tide.

I even respect you behind your back. I have a bad habit, when speaking of women while only men are present, of referring to women as bitches. This bitch this and this bitch that, you know. A while back I was speaking of you to a couple of cutthroats and I said, "this bitch . . ." And I felt very ashamed of myself about that. I passed judgment upon myself and suffered spiritually for days afterward. This may seem insignificant, but I attach great importance to it because of the chain of thought kicked off by it. I care about you, I am concerned about you, which is all very new for, and a sharp departure from, Eldridge X.

Your persistent query, "How can he tell? He has no choices," deserves an answer. But it is not the type of question that can be answered by words. It takes time and deeds, and this involves trust, it involves making ourselves vulnerable to each other, to strip ourselves naked, to become sitting ducks for each other—and if one of the ducks is shamming, then the sincere duck will pay in pain— but the deceitful duck, I feel, will be the loser. (If both ducks are shamming, what a lark, what a fiasco, what a put-on, what a despicable thought! I laugh at it because it has no power over me, I do not feel vulnerable to it, I feel protected by the flashing eyes of Portia. I extended my trust to you. I am vulnerable and defenseless and I make myself a duck for you.)

Listen: Your letter is very beautiful, and you came through with rockets on. You came through and landed on your feet, with spiked shoes on, right on my heart. It is not that we are making each other up and it is not ourselves alone who are involved in what is happening to us. It is really a complex movement taking place of which we are mere parts. We represent historical forces and it is really these forces that are coalescing and moving toward each other. And it is not a fraud, forced out of desperation. We live in a disoriented, deranged social structure, and we have transcended its barriers in our own ways and have stepped psychologically outside its madness and repressions. It is lonely out here. We recognize each other. And, having recognized each other, is it any wonder that our souls hold hands and cling together even while our minds equivocate, hesitate, vacillate, and tremble?

> Peace. Don't panic, and don't wake up.
> Dream on. I am
> Yours,
> *Eldridge*

IV:
White Woman,
Black Man

The Allegory
of the Black Eunuchs

I sat down to eat my beans at a table for four with two of my contemporaries: young, strong, superlative Black Eunuchs in the prime. Soon after we were seated, an old fat Lazarus, with sleek, grayish hair that had been artificially straightened and a jolly, ebullient smile which made him resemble a chocolate Santa Claus, invited himself over to our table and sat down in the chair opposite me. I exchanged glances with my contemporaries. Ironical smiles lit our black faces, while an intenser fire blazed in our eyes as we scrutinized this Lazarus interloper.

A few minutes passed in silence.

My contemporaries and I, we had a thing going about elderly Negroes like this one sitting opposite from me. There was something in his style, the way he carried himself, that we held in contempt. We had him written down as an Uncle Tom—not that we had ever seen him buck dancing or licking the white man's boots, but we knew that black rebels his age do not walk the streets in America: they were either dead, in prison, or in exile in another country. Or else, and this is how we sized this one up, they had turned into a type of fake that proliferates in the Negro ghetto. Not a passive resister (and he wasn't non-violent), he was death on another black, and although the white man had ripped off his whole existence, his whole race, he was always talking about what he would do if the white man ever did something to him personally. If talk alone could overthrow a government he would be in power. From a certain point of view we hated this black, but in a subtle way we were fascinated by the curious terms at which he had arrived with the world.

Just then, and with no apparent provocation, the young Eunuch on my left said, pounding his fist on the table for emphasis, "Old Lazarus, why come you're not dead?"

"What?" asked the Infidel, startled more by the suddenness of the question and the menacing tone in which it was hurled at him than by the question itself. (After all, his entire generation was being asked the same question in a million different guises: Charlie Parker asked Lester Young, Dizzy Gillespie asked Louis Armstrong, Mao Tse-tung asked Chiang Kai-shek, Fidel Castro asked Batista, Malcolm X asked Martin Luther King, Robert F. Williams asked Roy Wilkins, Norman Mailer asked the Totalitarian Squares.) The question sank in slowly, and as it did his Santa Claus smile dissolved, with a hint of panic, into a twitch at the left corner of his fat mouth. His dark, beady eyes darted from face to face.

"I asked you why aren't you dead?" repeated the Eunuch on my left.

"Why should *I* be dead? I don't under—"

"If you had laid down your life," the Eunuch cut him off, "at least we could respect you. At least we could say you were a man—a great man. At least we could point to your grave as a sign, a standard, with pride—*with reverence!* But no, you cringing cunctator, you dared to cling to your miserable life, to grow old and gray and fat and funky!" The Accuser broke off and started eating his beans with a vengeance, as though each bean were a white man, and he downed them by the spoonful.

"What's wrong with this cat today?" asked the Accused, his face screwed up in nervous bafflement.

"He's sick," I offered, to see how the Infidel would take it.

"He must be sick," said the Accused, stirring his coffee uncertainly. "All this stupid talk about death and dying."

"Yes, I'm sick!" erupted the Accuser, almost choking, talking through his beans. *"You* make me sick, Methuselah! What are you trying to do, win a longevity contest? How did you get that gray hair—how did you manage to survive? Yeah. I'm sick, sick, sick!"

"I'm sick, too," said the Eunuch on my right, speaking for the first time. "I'm sick, sick, sick!"

"I'm sick, too," I said.

"What's the name of this game?" asked Lazarus, trying to inject a note of levity, on the sly. "This is a new one on me."

It was a cruel thing we were doing and we knew it because we had done it before to others. In one sense we were only playing with him, probing him, examining him, studying him, but on another level we were deadly serious. The Lazarus, detecting the ambiguity, was confused.

"Do you know the difference between a *gorilla* and a *guerrilla?*" the Eunuch on my right asked the Accused.

The Accused appeared to be contemplating an answer.

"I'll make it easy for you," the Eunuch said. "You're a gorilla, and a guerrilla is everything you are not."

The Accused opened his mouth to reply, but the Eunuch on my left, who had cast the first stone, cut him off. "A guerrilla is a man," he snapped, his eyes flashing, "but you're some kind of freak!"

A self-searching, inward-looking silence ensued. One thought of blood and guns and knives, whips, ropes and chains and trees, screams, night riders, fear, nightsticks,

police dogs and firehoses, fire, wounds and bombs, old
women in pain and young women defiled, lies, jeers, little
boys frozen in their first heat and young men destudded and
old men burnt out, little girls psychically vitiated and physically massacred . . .

After a while I asked the Accused, in a neutral voice,
"Have you ever hit a black woman?"

As if his switch had been flipped, his eyes lit up and, anxious for what in his death he took to be a change of subject,
the Lazarus took the bait. The twinkle in his eye turned evil
as he leaned across the table and said, in a confidential
way: "I wish I had a nickle for every bitch whose ass I've
put my foot in! I'd be so rich right now that you lames
would have to put in your requests six months in advance
just to get to see me, let alone sit down at the same table
with me!"

"A home-run slash at your neck with a scimitar is the solution to all your problems, Lazarus!" hissed the Accuser,
the Eunuch on my left, his lips trembling with rage.

"What do you mean by that?" asked the Accused, affecting not to have understood.

"He means what I mean," said the Eunuch on my right,
"that for four hundred years you have had the fear of the
slavemaster in you, but now it's time for you to know the
fear of your own kind!"

"Humph!" snorted the Accused, and he took a spoonful
of beans into his mouth, chewing them absently. He re-
sumed talking after a few moments. "Black women take
kindness for weakness. Leave them the least little opening
and they will put you on the cross. I hate a black bitch.
You can't trust them like white women, and if you try to,
they won't appreciate it and they won't know how to act.
It would be like trying to pamper a cobra. Anyway, every
black woman secretly hates black men. Secretly, they all

love white men—some of them will tell you so to your face, the others will tell you by their deeds and actions. Haven't you ever noticed that just as soon as a black woman becomes successful she marries a white man? I'm going by what I know. I know one black bitch who always says that there ain't nothing a black man can do for her except leave her alone or bring her a message from, or carry a message to, a white man.

"There is no love left between a black man and a black woman. Take me, for instance. I love white women and hate black women. It's just in me, so deep that I don't even try to get it out of me any more. I'd jump over ten nigger bitches just to get to one white woman. Ain't no such thing as an ugly white woman. A white woman is beautiful even if she's baldheaded and only has one tooth. . . . It's not just the fact that she's a woman that I love; I love her skin, her soft, smooth, white skin. I like to just lick her white skin as if sweet, fresh honey flows from her pores, and just to touch her long, soft, silky hair. There's a softness about a white woman, something delicate and soft inside her. But a nigger bitch seems to be full of steel, granite-hard and resisting, not soft and submissive like a white woman. Ain't nothing more beautiful than a white woman's hair being blown by the wind. The white woman is more than a woman to me. . . . She's like a goddess, a symbol. My love for her is religious and beyond fulfillment. I worship her. I love a white woman's dirty drawers.

"Sometimes I think that the way I feel about white women, I must have inherited from my father and his father and his father's father—as far back as you can go into slavery. I must have inherited from all those black men part of my desire for the white woman, because I have more love for her than one man should have. Yes, I want all the white women that they wanted but were never able to get. They passed on their desire to me, they must have; desire for the white woman is like a cancer eating my heart out and devouring my brain. In my dreams I see white women jumping over a fence like dainty little lambs, and every time one of them jumps over, her hair just catches the breeze and splays out behind her like a mane on a Palomino stallion: blondes, redheads, brunettes, strawberry blondes, dirty blondes, drugstore blondes, platinum blondes—all of them. They are the things in my nightmares. Does all this sound like I'm making it up, youngblood?"

He nodded at me; he was asking me. I took my time about answering. I would have preferred to remain silent. I said, "Why should you lie to us? I mean, no one can be completely true in all that they say, and you give me the impression of, well, talking off the top of your head . . ."

He was laughing inside, I could see it in his eyes. Then he said, "Well, I've thought about it for years. You have to try to understand what's bugging you, you know. But really, I don't believe that I understand anything about anything, when you get right down to it. But I'm stuck with myself and I accept my own thoughts about things. For instance, I don't know just how it works, I mean I can't analyze it, but I know that the white man made the black woman the symbol of slavery and the white woman the symbol of freedom. Every time I embrace a black woman I'm embracing slavery, and when I put my arms around a white woman, well, I'm hugging freedom. The white man forebade me to have the white woman on pain of death. Literally, if I touched a white woman it would cost me my life. Men die for freedom, but black men die for white women, who are the symbol of freedom. That was the white man's will, and as long as he has the power to enforce his will upon me, force me to submit to his will in this instance or in any other, I will not be free. I will not be free until the day I can have a white woman in my bed and a white man minds his own business. Until that day comes, my entire existence is tainted, poisoned, and I will still be a slave—and so will the white woman.

"You may not believe this . . . when I off a nigger bitch, I close my eyes and concentrate real hard, and pretty soon I get to believing that I'm riding one of them bucking blondes. I tell you the truth, that's the only way that I can bust my nuts with a black bitch, to close my eyes and pretend that she is Jezebel. If I was to look down and see a black bitch underneath me or if my hand happened to feel her nappy hair, that would be the end, it would be all over. I might as well get on up and split because I wouldn't be able to get anything down, even if I piled her all night long. Any black man who says he don't dig Jezebel is a goddam liar. I believe that if a leader wanted to unite the Negroes in a solid unity, he could do so very easily. All he'd have to do is promise every black man a white woman and every black woman a white man. He would have so many followers that he wouldn't know what to do with them all. Believe me.

"I'm going to tell you three youngbloods something that I don't like to talk about. I don't like to talk about none of this shit. . . . You cats are setting here all puffed up. You think you got a hell of a thing going for yourselves, but you don't really know anything about yourselves, or about your women, or about white people. You probably won't believe what I tell you: it rubs your ego the wrong way. But I'm going to tell you anyway."

The Lazarus paused and squirmed around in his chair as though trying to get a better grip on it with his rump. When he spoke again there was a tremor in his voice: "He who worships the Virgin Mary will lust for the beautiful dumb blonde. And she who yearns to be rocked in the arms of Jesus will burn for the blue eyes and white arms of the All-American Boy."

Here the Lazarus stopped and searched our faces. But

our faces were impenetrable masks and we gave him no
sign. He went on: "The war going on between the black
man and the white man is not the only war. Life is full of
little wars and you fight them all at the same time. You
have to have a grand strategy designed to cope with all
hostilities, you have to have a style, and if there is someone
making war on you and you don't know it, well, you are in
big trouble, you're lost from the go. . . . There is a war
going on between the black man and the black woman,
which makes her the silent ally, indirectly but effectively, of
the white man. The black woman is an unconsenting ally
and she may not even realize it—but the white man sure
does. That's why, all down through history, he has propped
her up economically above you and me, to strengthen her
hand against us. But the white man is a fool because he is
also fighting a war against the white woman. And it doesn't
end there: white men have a war going on against each
other.

"The myth of the strong black woman is the other side of
the coin of the myth of the beautiful dumb blonde. The
white man turned the white woman into a weak-minded,
weak-bodied, delicate freak, a sex pot, and placed her on a
pedestal; he turned the black woman into a strong self-
reliant Amazon and deposited her in his kitchen—that's the
secret of Aunt Jemima's bandanna. The white man turned
himself into the Omnipotent Administrator and established
himself in the Front Office. And he turned the black man
into the Supermasculine Menial and kicked him out into the
fields. The white man wants to be the *brain* and he wants us
to be the muscle, the *body*. All this is tied up together in a
crazy way which was never too clear to me. At one time it
seems absolutely clear and at other times I don't believe in
it. It reminds me of two sets of handcuffs that have all four
of us tied up together, holding all black and white flesh in a

certain mold. This is why, when you get down to the root of it, the white man doesn't want the black man, the black woman, or the white woman to have a higher education. Their enlightenment would pose a threat to his omnipotence.

"Haven't you ever wondered why the white man genuinely applauds a black man who achieves excellence with his body in the field of sports, while he hates to see a black man achieve excellence with his brain? The mechanics of the myth demand that the Brain and the Body, like east and west, must never meet—especially in competition on the same level. When it comes to the mechanics of the myth, the Brain and the Body are mutually exclusive. There can be no true competition between superiors and inferiors. This is why it has been so hard historically for Negroes to break the color bar in sport after sport. Once the color bar falls, the magic evaporates, and when the black man starts to excel in a particular sport the question starts floating around: 'Is boxing dying?' 'Is baseball through?' 'What happened to football?' 'What is basketball coming to?' In fact, the new symbol of white supremacy is golf, because there the Brain dominates the Body. But just as soon as the Body starts ripping off a few trophies, they will be asking the question, 'What happened to golf?'

"All this became clear when Joe Louis cleaned out Max Schmeling in their second fight. Schmeling stood for the very thing the white man nursed and worshiped in his own heart. But the whites applauded Joe for crushing Schmeling. Why? Because Joe's victory over Schmeling symbolized the triumph of capitalistic democracy over nazism? No! There may have been a little of that to it, but on a deeper level they applauded Joe for the same reason they despised Ingemar Johansson, while rewarding him handsomely, for knocking out Floyd Patterson. Joe's victory over Schmeling confirmed, while Floyd's defeat contradicted, the white man's image of the black man as the Supermasculine Menial, the personification of mindless brute force, the perfect slave. And Sonny Liston, the mindless Body, is preferred over loud-mouthed Cassius Clay, because, after all, it takes at least a birdbrain to run a loud mouth, and the white man despises even that much brain in a black man. And when Clay, the loud-mouthed clown, abdicates his image as the Body and becomes Muhammad Ali, the Brain, whitey can't hold his mud! The white man loves the Supermasculine Menial—John Henry, the steel-driving man, all Body, driven to his knees by the Machine, which is the phallus symbol of the Brain and the ultimate ideal of the Omnipotent Administrator. To the white man's way of thinking, this was a perfect system of social imagery. But like all perfect systems, it had a great big flaw right in the middle of it.

"The Omnipotent Administrator conceded to the Supermasculine Menial all of the attributes of masculinity associated with the Body: strength, brute power, muscle, even the beauty of the brute body. Except one. There was this single attribute of masculinity which he was unwilling to relinquish, even though this particular attribute is the essence and seat of masculinity: sex. The penis. The black man's penis was the monkey wrench in the white man's perfect machine. The penis, virility, is of the Body. It is not of the Brain: the Brain is neuter, *HOMO, MACHINE.* But in the deal which the white man forced upon the black man, the black man was given the Body as his domain while the white man preempted the Brain for himself. By and by, the Omnipotent Administrator discovered that in the fury of his scheming he had blundered and clipped himself of his penis (notice the puny image the white man has of his own penis. He calls it a 'prick,' a 'peter,' a 'pecker'). So he reneged on the bargain. He called the Supermasculine Menial back and said: 'Look, Boy, we have a final little adjustment to make. I'm still going to be the Brain and you're still the Body. But from now on, you do all the flexing but I'll do all the fucking. The Brain must control the Body. To prove my omnipotence I must cuckold you and fetter your bull balls. I will fetter the range of your rod and limit its reach. My prick will excel your rod. I have made a calculation. I will have sexual freedom. But I will bind your rod with my omnipotent will, and place a limitation on its aspiration which you will violate on pain of death. . . . I will have access to the white woman and I will have access to the black woman. The black woman will have access to you— but she will also have access to me. I forbid you access to the white woman. The white woman will have access to me, the Omnipotent Administrator, but I deny her access to you, you, the Supermasculine Menial. By subjecting your manhood to the control of my will, I shall control you. The stem of the Body, the penis, must submit to the will of the Brain.'

"It was the perfect solution, only it didn't work. It only drove the truth underground. You can't really dissociate the penis from the Body! Not even the Brain, the Omnipotent Administrator, can do that! *But you can seize the Body in a rage, in violent and hateful frustration at this one great flaw in a perfect plan, this monkey wrench in a perfect machine, string the Body from the nearest tree and pluck its strange fruit, its big Nigger dick, pickle it in a bottle and take it home to the beautiful dumb blonde and rejoice in the lie that not the Body but the Brain is the man.*"

The Lazarus stopped talking and sat there with his mouth hanging open. He was breathing hard, as if he had been running and was out of breath. The Eunuch on my left was staring off into space, looking off deliberately rather than allow anyone to see the wild look I knew would be in his eyes. Thought refused to crystallize in my mind; I poured more coffee into my cup, and as I lifted the cup to my lips I blew softly on the surface of the murky brew to cool it off, and stared over the rim at the Infidel, who sat with his face screwed up, biting his ample bottom lip, as if he was trying hard to remember something or maybe to understand or figure something out. He seemed embarrassed. The Eunuch on my right was staring down into his plate of beans.

Then the Infidel looked up and locked my eyes with his own. A cruel, wounded expression was in his eyes. I could see a pain there that was dreadful. It made me feel fear— not so much for the Infidel as for myself, my generation, my contemporaries, because I was not sure that I, we, knew what to do or would learn before it was too late, and would be able to escape from feeling that same deep-seated pain some day, myself, ourselves. It seemed to me in that moment, and I knew that the same thought was running through the minds of my Eunuch contemporaries, that any fate, death, the gas chamber, the electric chair, a firing squad, heroin, suicide—anything would be better than to submit to the terrible, horrible pain which the Infidel had learned to live with. I felt a hot throbbing in my crotch. Instinctively and with a taste of panic, I reached down, almost afraid that my rod would be missing, but it was there and it was erect and I squeezed it and it was strong and resilient and firm. When I gave it that squeeze, a wave of strength surged through my body. I felt powerful, and I knew that I would make it if I never betrayed the law of my rod. The Infidel smiled, and I was sure he had read my thoughts. He let out a deep breath and sat back in his chair and started talking in a tired voice, almost a monotone:

"I had a woman once—no, *a bitch!*—who had a hook

like Sugar Ray Robinson. I had to knock her out every Saturday night. She'd start an argument and then tee off on me, just like a man. How're you supposed to treat a bitch who can't live with you without fighting? And she didn't have to be mad at me to start a fight. I experimented with her. I tried all kinds of technique on her. Once I refused to argue with her. I just stood there and looked at her in a way that she knew that I was not mad at her, as if I was saying to her, 'Look, baby, it's up to you. Whatever happens will be because you made it happen.' *BOOM!* She hit me in the mouth. That was when I realized that she could not accept me as a man unless I acted like the Body, exerting physical force over her. I didn't hit her back. I was filled with a rage that I had never felt before or since. Actually, I think I went momentarily insane. I grabbed her by her arm, whipped out my switchblade knife—it had about an eight-inch blade—I opened my knife and made her sit on the sofa. I could see that she thought it was all over for her. Her eyes were big as a cow's and she was really scared. I shoved the knife into her hand and made her take it. Then I lay down with my arms around her body and with my head in her lap. She was furious. She threatened to cut my jugular vein if I did not get up. I was not my usual self and I had no intention of getting up. It seemed that if I got up I would not be able to live another second. That was the feeling I had, that if I got up and let her go or tried to protect myself in any way from the knife, I could not go on living. So I laid there with my jugular vein exposed to her and the knife. And I went to sleep. At first she tried to get my head out of her lap, then she stopped that, then she started crying. I could feel the sobs racking her body. But I kept my eyes closed and went to sleep. I had no dream or anything. It was a deep, peaceful, sweet sleep. I can still recall the ecstasy of that sleep. I have never in my life experienced such blissful sleep. When I woke up, she was holding my head cradled in her lap and she had a beautiful, saintly glow on her face, an expression that was utterly foreign to anything that I had ever seen in her before. Then I remembered the knife and a great fear came over me. I jumped up and looked around. She had closed up the knife and broken the blade and thrown it across the room on the floor. My stomach trembled as I realized what a big chance I had taken.

"Anyway, we went along fine for about a month. Our relationship was infused with new life and vitality. During that time we did not have a single argument, not a single harsh word passed between us. That granite, that steel (which I hate in a black bitch!) was gone. And strangely, I felt myself acting natural, without pretense toward her. It seemed as if we were dancing through those days perfectly in time and in step with each other. Then one day, we were out driving and I ran through a red light just a little too late and this motorcycle cop pulled me over.

" 'Say, Boy,' he said to me, 'are you color-blind?' I didn't want a ticket so I decided to talk him out of it. I went into my act, gave him a big smile and explained to him that I was awfully sorry, that I thought that I could make it but that my old car was too slow. He talked real bad to me, took me on a long trip about how important it was that I obeyed the laws and regulations and how else can a society be controlled and administered without obedience to the law. I said a bunch of Yes Sir's and No Sir's and he told me to run along and be a good boy. When I drove off, I looked over at my woman and she had turned completely sour. That sweetness of the last month was gone and I could see the granite and steel in her. When we got home she tried to start a fight with me, but I refused to respond. Without another word, she packed up all her belongings and split. The bitch cut me clean aloose. I've never been cut loose that clean before! She got herself another stud. They used to fight all up and down the streets. That stud used to love to fight her just as much as she loved to fight. They were very happy together. Later on, she killed that cat. Shot him down in the street like a dog—and she beat the case in court. They called it justifiable homicide.

"Then the bitch changed her name and started singing professionally. She made it real big, her name and picture was in all the magazines and newspapers. I used to go check her performances in night clubs. She was great. She made a lot of big money. Then guess what she did. She married a white man! The cat was a blank, a tramp, he didn't have anything going for himself. He didn't have a quarter when he married her. She gave him all of her money. He ran through her bank account. He bought himself a big fancy night club. Then he divorced her. She lost her touch after that and started slipping down, down, down. Her earning power shrank to nothing. She hung the whole life up and started singing church music. Spirituals. She joined a church, became real religious. Everybody said she fell in love with Jesus and that in him she finally found her righteous man. That's where she is right now, in that church.

"Ever since then I always believed that marrying a white man, to a black woman, is like adding the final star to her crown. It's the apex of achievement in her eyes and in the eyes of her sisters. Look at how many famous black celebrities marry white men. All of the Negro women who are not celebrities wish they were so that they, too, could marry white men. Whitey is their dream boy. When they kiss you it ain't really you they're kissing. They close their eyes and picture their white dream boy. Listen to the grapevine . . . Jesus Christ the pure is the black woman's psychic bridegroom. You will learn before you die that during coition and at the moment of her orgasm, the black woman, in the first throes of her spasm, shouts out the name of Jesus. 'Oh, Jesus, I'm coming!' she shouts to him. And to you it will hurt. It will be like a knife in your heart. It will be the same as if your woman, during orgasm, calls out the name of some sneaky cat who lives down the block.

"Now there is one thing I want to tell you that is directly related to this. To be sure, I have never understood it and I don't believe that I ever will. But I have seen it work and it may be that you brothers can understand it, and it may prove useful to you, it may help you to make it. There is a sickness in the whites that lies at the core of their madness and this sickness makes them act in many different ways. But there is one way it makes some of them act that seems to contradict everything we know about whitey and shakes many blacks up when they first encounter it. . . . There are white men who will pay you to fuck their wives. They approach you and say, 'How would you like to fuck a white woman?' 'What is this?' you ask. 'On the up-and-up,' he assures you. 'It's all right. She's my wife. She needs black rod, is all. She has to have it. It's like a medicine or drug to her. She has to have it. I'll pay you. It's all on the level, no trick involved. Interested?' You go with him and he drives you to their home. The three of you go into the bedroom. There is a certain type who will leave you and his wife alone and tell you to pile her real good. After it is all over, he will pay you and drive you to wherever you want to go. Then there are some who like to peep at you through a key-hole and watch you have his woman, or peep at you through a window, or lie under the bed and listen to the creaking of the bed as you work out. There is another type who likes to masturbate while he stands beside the bed and watches you pile her. There is the type who likes to eat his woman up after you get through piling her. And there is the type who only wants you to pile her for a little while, just long enough to thaw her out and kick her motor over and arouse her to heat, then he wants you to jump off real quick and he will jump onto her and together they can make it from there by themselves."

It did not occur to me to say anything; I didn't know what to say. I was angry at the Infidel and repulsed by his monologue and the importance he seemed to attach to these matters. My dreams lay elsewhere and I could not begin to evaluate the things he had been talking about. I sat there, savoring the strange quality of the emotion which had been aroused within me. I don't know when the Eunuch on my left started to speak, for I first became aware of his voice as sound purely, a nebulous, incoherent sound, and only later did I begin to distinguish the words:

". . . fed up with it! You old Lazarus. Everything you said was twisted, it was all dead and stinking, it was all warped and out of joint, it was off cue, off center." The Eunuch had his jaw set defiantly.

"Yes, I know," said the Infidel, "and you youngbloods see your big chance coming up to change all of that. Every man with a pipe dream sees his chance as just coming. . . . But even so, you have to admit that the white man is a bitch with his shit. Did he clean us out or not, huh? Did he take care of business? He took care of so much business that it got good to him, and he got carried away and cleaned everybody out—including himself. Now ain't that a motherfucking shame?" The Infidel looked from one to the other of us. No one replied to him. We just stared at him, at his face, his eyes, his smooth chocolate skin. Then he broke out laughing, until his obese frame shook. There was no telling what he was laughing at. It was coming from deep inside him, but his face looked pained, as if he were not enjoying his laugh. Several times he tried to say something but each time he was overcome by laughter. Finally he blurted out: ". . . you've got to give the devil his due," and went into another spasm of chuckles and grunts.

When the laughter died he began drumming on the table with his short, fat fingers. "I had a very close friend once," he said. "We grew up together—never mind where. He was the best friend I ever had, closer than a brother. We were tighter than fish pussy, and that's waterproof. When we were just kids, we took a blood-brother oath, like Indian braves. Just me and him. We made a pact to be lifelong comrades." His mind drifted for a moment. Tiny drops of perspiration stood out on his forehead. "But something happened and I . . . I . . . went away . . . I didn't see or hear of him for many, many years. Then, finally, I went back . . . to that place. I had to see the old hometown once more. I decided to look up my old friend. After searching for him, it turned out that he was in an institution. A mental institution. He had been there ever since—for all those years. So I went to see him. He had changed completely, so much that I don't believe I would have recognized him, if it were not for his eyes. I'd never forget those eyes, never. He had eyes like they say Jomo Kenyatta has, look right through a brick wall." The Infidel lifted his hand and pointed at the Eunuch on my left. "My friend had his eyes, only more so, just like this brother here," he said. An embarrassed, frightened look showed on his face for a moment, which he quickly suppressed. The Eunuch on my left shifted about in his chair.

"But he recognized me, my friend did," said the Infidel. "Immediately he knew who I was. He didn't have to pull me from his memory, as you'd think he would have after all those years. The minute they brought him into the visiting room I could see that he recognized me, though he didn't call my name. We sat down at a little table and he said to me: 'Ah! I thought you would never get here! Now we can embark on our great enterprise! We will transform the whole of proud Europe into an international whorehouse, and men from all over the earth will make their pilgrimage there and fertilize the depleted human soil with their rich and varied seed!' I said nothing to him, couldn't say anything. I just listened. He talked on and on. He took me back, back, back. Then it was time for me to go. I promised him I'd be back the next day. They led him away. I never went back. Even as I promised him, I knew I would never return, never." The Infidel paused, swallowed. He was struggling with himself, fighting to keep under control something powerful, torrential, within himself. You could feel the terrible force of the agony raging inside him. "He died two weeks later, my friend did—from self-inflicted wounds, from banging his own head against a jagged edge of a concrete wall."

For many minutes no one spoke. Each was submerged in thoughts of his own. Finally, the Eunuch on my left, in a cold, icy tone, said:

"You dirty Lazarus. You killed him. You murdered him. You betrayed him!"

The Infidel made as if to reply, but the effort died. The Eunuch on my left said to the Infidel:

"Your trouble, old Lazarus, is that you can't stand the sight of the slavemaster's blood."

The Infidel looked surprised. "The world," he said slowly, "cannot stand another bloodbath."

"The world is hemophiliac," retorted the Eunuch. "Look at it! When did the world ever stop bleeding? It never has, for a moment, ceased to bleed; it's bleeding somewhere right this very moment. Right now, as we sit here talking, someone somewhere is taking careful aim at someone else, at an enemy. Someone is thrusting with a blade, at an enemy. Someone is lighting a fuse, at an enemy. In Africa, Asia, Europe, South America, and right here in the good old U.S.A., blood is flowing. Go listen to the radio or TV right now and the first news you catch will be of blood, a count of the bodies. Go pick up a newspaper or magazine and it will be dripping with blood. Blood flows from the TV screen. So why does it shock you to hear of blood?"

"Yes, the world is bleeding," said the Infidel, "but it's bleeding to death. How much longer can it last?" He shuddered at his own question.

"Blood is a lubricant," said the Eunuch on my left. "It smooths the way and enables a people to slip out of the tightest of clutches. You don't tinker with a logjam, man, you dynamite it!"

"You are thirsty for blood!" said the Infidel, speaking directly to the Eunuch on my left. "But it won't do!"

"Yes!" replied the Eunuch. "I'm thirsty for blood—white man's blood. And when I drink I want to drink deeply, because I have a deep thirst to quench. I want to drink for every black man, woman, and child dragged to the slaughter from the shores of Africa, for every one of my brothers and sisters who suffered helplessly in the rotten holds of the damned slave ships—for your friend who bashed his own brains out in that nuthouse—I want to drink the white man's blood for every ounce of my flesh and blood that he crushed and broke in the Caribbean Islands, for all the souls of black folk mangled in the fetid fields of the Old South and for every one slaughtered and lynched in the mire of the New South—and in the North, East, and West of the hells of North America! Only the white man's blood can wash away the pain I feel. You shrink from shedding the white man's blood, you old Lazarus, but I say to you that the day is here when I will march into the Mississippi legislature with a blazing machine gun in my hands and a pocketful of grenades. Since I will be going to die, I definitely will be going to kill."

"No," said the Infidel. "No. More blood will only add crime upon crime. No!" He suddenly stood up from the table, looked at each of us as if to plead, like a criminal before a jury he knows is about to send him to the death chamber. He breathed deeply as he had done earlier, and let his shoulders sag. "Blood upon blood; crime upon crime; brick of blood upon brick of blood of a new mad Tower of Babel which, too, will fall. . . . There can be no triumph in blood." Then he turned and faltered slowly away from the table.

We watched him walk away. He stopped and looked back at us, as if he half-expected, half-hoped, for us to call him back. Then he turned and faded from our sight, from our lives.

The Primeval Mitosis

And the Lord God caused a deep sleep to fall upon Adam, and he slept: and he took one of his ribs, and closed up the flesh instead thereof; And the rib, which the Lord God had taken from man, made he a woman, and brought her unto the man. And Adam said, This is now bone of my bones, and flesh of my flesh: she shall be called Woman, because she was taken out of Man.

—Genesis 2:21–23

It is as if in the evolution of sex a particle one day broke away from an X-chromosome, and thereafter in relation to X-chromosomes could produce only an incomplete female—the creature we now call the male! It is to this original chromosomal deficiency that all the various troubles to which the male falls heir can be traced.

Ashley Montagu,
The Natural Superiority of Women

I think that *any* submerged class is going to be more accustomed to sexuality than a leisure class. A leisure class may be more *preoccupied* with sexuality; but a submerged class is going to be more drenched in it.

You see, the upper classes are obsessed with sex, but they contain very little of it themselves. They use up much too much sex in their manipulations of power. In effect, they exchange sex for power. So they restrict themselves in their sexuality—

176

whereas the submerged classes have to take their desires for power and plow them back into sex.

Norman Mailer
The Presidential Papers

The roots of heterosexuality are buried in that evolutionary choice made long ago in some misty past—but not so remote that it can't be reached with the long arm of the mind—by some unknown forerunner of Homo sapiens. Struggling up from some murky swamp, some stagnant mudhole, some peaceful meadow, that unknown ancestor of Man/Woman, by some weird mitosis of the essence, divided its Unitary Self in half—into the male and female hemispheres of the Primeval Sphere. These hemispheres evolved into what we know today as man and woman.

When the Primeval Sphere divided itself, it established a basic tension of attraction, a dynamic magnetism of opposites—the Primeval Urge—which exerts an irresistible attraction between the male and female hemispheres, ever tending to fuse them back together into a unity in which the male and female realize their true nature—the lost unity of the Primeval Sphere. This is the eternal and unwavering motivation of the male and female hemispheres, of man and woman, to transcend the Primeval Mitosis and achieve supreme identity in the Apocalyptic Fusion.

Each half of the human equation, the male and female hemispheres of the Primeval Sphere, must prepare themselves for the fusion by achieving a Unitary Sexual Image, i.e., a heterosexual identity free from the mutually exclusive, antagonistic, antipodal impediments of homosexuality (the product of the fissure of society into antagonistic classes and a dying culture and civilization alienated from its biology).

Man's continual striving for a Unitary Sexual Image,

which can only be achieved in a Unitary Society, becomes a basic driving force of the Class Struggle, which is, in turn, the dynamic of history. The quest for the Apocalyptic Fusion will find optimal conditions only in a Classless Society, the absence of classes being the *sine qua non* for the existence of a Unitary Society in which the Unitary Sexual Image can be achieved.

Each social structure projects onto the screen of possibility the images of the highest type of male and female sexual identities realizable within the limits of that society. The people within that society are motivated and driven, by the perennial quest for Apocalyptic Fusion, to achieve this highest identity, or as close as they can come to the perfection of the Unitary Sexual Image. All impediments to realization of this image become sources of alienation, obstacles in the way of the Self seeking to realize its ultimate identity.

Since each society projects its own sexual image, the Unitary Society will project a Unitary Sexual Image. We can thus postulate, following the model of Marx, that in ancient communal society, which was not cleft into antagonistic classes, there existed a Unitary Society in which a Unitary Sexual Image was in natural coincidence with the way of life of the people. This is the lost innocence of the Garden of Eden.

The Class Society projects a fragmented sexual image. Each class projects a sexual image coinciding with its class-function in society. And since its class-function will differ from that of other classes, its sexual image will differ also and in the same proportion. The source of the fragmentation of the Self in Class Society lies in the alienation between the function of man's Mind and the function of his Body. Man as thinker performs an Administrative Function in society. Man as doer performs a Brute Power Function. These two basic functions I symbolize, when they are embodied in living men functioning in society, as the Omnipotent Administrator and the Supermasculine Menial.

Since all men are created equal, when the Self is fragmented by the operation of the laws and forces of Class Society, men in the elite classes usurp the controlling and Administrative Function of the society as a whole—i.e., they usurp the administrative component in the nature and biology of the men in the classes below them. Administrative power is concentrated at the apex of society, in the Godhead of the society (pharaoh, king, president, chairman). Administrative power beneath the apex is delegated. Those in classes to which no administrative power has been delegated have the administrative component in their personalities suppressed, alienated, denied expression. Those who have usurped the Administrative Function we shall call the Omnipotent Administrators. Struggling among themselves for higher positions in the administrative hierarchy, they repudiate the component of Brute Power in themselves, claim no kinship with it, and project it onto the men in the classes below them.

All the males in the classes beneath *the* Omnipotent Administrator, or Godhead of the society, are alienated from the administrative component in themselves in proportion to their distance from the apex. That is, they perceive their alienation in terms of their distance from the apex. This perception of their alienation, in terms of the apex, is an illusion. In fact, their alienation must be measured by their distance from the attainment of a Unitary Sexual Image, the take-off stage for the Apocalyptic Fusion. Generally, in a fragmented Class Society, the basic impulse of Omnipotent Administrators is to despise their bodies and glorify their minds.

Those who have been assigned the Brute Power Function

we shall call the Supermasculine Menials. They are alienated from their minds. For them the mind counts only insofar as it enables them to receive, understand, and carry out the will of the Omnipotent Administrators.

The Class Society has a built-in bias, which tends to perpetuate the social system. The Omnipotent Administrators, wishing to preserve what they perceive as their superior position and way of life, have, from a class point of view and also on an individual level, a negative reaction toward any influence in the society that tends to increase the number of males qualified to fulfill the functions of administration. When it comes to anything that will better the lot of those beneath him, the Omnipotent Administrator starts with a basic "anti" reflex. Any liberality he might show is an indication of the extent to which he has suppressed his "anti" reflex, and is itself a part of his lust for omnipotence. His liberality is, in fact, charity.

The Supermasculine Menial clearly realizes that the superiority of the Omnipotent Administrators over him is based upon the development of their minds and the power they command as a result. Hence, he starts with a "pro" reflex. He is, for example, pro-universal education at public expense.

Weakness, frailty, cowardice, and effeminacy are, among other attributes, associated with the Mind. Strength, brute power, force, virility, and physical beauty are associated with the Body. Thus the upper classes, or Omnipotent Administrators, are perennially associated with physical weakness, decay, underdeveloped bodies, effeminacy, sexual impotence, and frigidity. Virility, strength, and power are associated with the lower classes, the Supermasculine Menials.

In feudal society, the men of the nobility, who were Omnipotent Administrators by Divine Right, are generally considered to have been weak, delicate, and effeminate, with the affectations of demonstrative homosexuals. The serfs and peasants are considered to have been physically strong, sturdy, hearty, fecund—"supermasculine."

The image of the Omnipotent Administrator, that he is markedly effeminate and delicate by reason of his explicit repudiation and abdication of his body in preference for his mind, is decisive for the image of the woman of the elite classes. *Even though her man is effeminate, she is required to possess and project an image that is in sharp contrast to his, more sharply feminine than his, so that the effeminate image of her man can still, by virtue of the sharp contrast in degrees of femininity, be perceived as masculine.* Therefore, she becomes "Ultrafeminine."

In order to project an image of Ultrafemininity, the women of the elite repudiate and abdicate the Domestic Function of the female (which is, in the female, the counterpart of the function of Brute Power in the male). To enhance her image and to increase her femininity, the domestic component of her nature is projected onto the women in the classes beneath her, and the femininity of the women below is correspondingly decreased. In effect, a switch is made: the woman of the elite absorbs into her being the femininity of the woman below her, and she extirpates her domestic component; the woman below absorbs the elite woman's cast-off domestic component and relinquishes her own femininity. The elite woman thus becomes *Ultrafeminine* while the woman below becomes *Subfeminine.* For the purposes of social imagery, the woman below becomes an Amazon.

Thus, a most weird and complex dialectic of inversion is established in Class Society. The Omnipotent Administrator is launched on a perpetual search for his alienated body, for affirmation of his unstable masculinity. He becomes a worshiper of physical prowess, or he may come to despise the body and everything associated with it. Fearing impotence, impotence being implicit in his negation and abdication of his Body, his profoundest need is for evidence of his virility. His opposite, the Body, the Supermasculine Menial, is a threat to his self-concept (and to compound it all, this perceived threat and resultant fear is reinforced decisively by the fact that the men beneath him are a threat to him *in reality,* because their life goal is to destroy his Omnipotence over them). He views them as his enemies and inferiors, men of a lesser breed than himself and his kind. He despises, hates them. Yet, because of the infirmity in his image and being which moves him to worship masculinity and physical prowess, the Omnipotent Administrator cannot help but covertly, and perhaps in an extremely sublimated guise, envy the bodies and strength of the most alienated men beneath him—those furthest from the apex of administration—because the men most alienated from the mind, least diluted by admixture of the Mind, will be perceived as the most masculine manifestations of the Body: the Supermasculine Menials. (This is precisely the root, the fountainhead, of the homosexuality that is perennially associated with the Omnipotent Administrator.) The dialectic of the Supermasculine Menial is the converse of that of the Omnipotent Administrator. The Supermasculine Menial has an infirmity of the brain because of his alienation from his mind.

Because he despises weakness of the body in himself, the Omnipotent Administrator will have a secret or subconscious aversion to the women of his own class, because of the Ultrafemininity which they have developed to counterbalance his effeminacy. At the same time, he will surpass himself in his efforts to conceal his aversion and make believe that the very opposite is true. He thus makes an icon of his woman and, literally, worships her. He pays obeisance to Her ritualistically while in the chapel of Her presence. Enshrining Her on a pedestal, he goes off seeking confirmation of his insecure masculinity elsewhere. Since the women of the elite tend to become the same, i.e., to project a homogeneous image of Ultrafemininity, they cannot, in the end, satisfy his psychic need—the confirmation of his masculinity. Strength gauges its own potency through a confrontation with other strength. To test it, he must go where it is. He may become addicted to a masculine-imaged sport, become a big-game hunter, outdoorsman, mountain climber. He may find satisfaction enough from some outlet as to have no problem at all which he is aware of as a sexual infirmity. He may be unaware of his impotence because he is blinded by his dazzling success and superiority in another field.

But in his quest for confirmation of his masculinity, a quest which he usually perceives as a search for sexual satisfaction and new conquests, his attention is attracted, with the force of the pull of gravity, to the potent Bodies in the classes beneath him, to the strength. He may sexually exploit the white-collar Bodies at the office; then, on his descent toward the Power Source, he may be drawn to the blue-collar Bodies in the plant. If these Bodies leave him still in the clutches of his lust and insecurity, he will bore deeper and deeper into the lower strata until he finds his sexual Balm of Gilead. There is a Pandora's box of sexual aberrations here.

The Body is tropical, warm, hot: Fire! It is soft, pleasing to the touch, luscious to the kiss. The blood is hot. Muscles are strength. *The basic motion of the women of the elite is flight from their bodies.* The weakness of the female body when contrasted to the strength of the male body is an obvious attribute of femininity as manifested in social imagery. Thus, to enhance and emphasize the femininity of her image—which is mandatory in order that she present a sharp feminine contrast to the effeminate image of her man, the Omnipotent Administrator—she seeks to increase the weakness of her body and stamp out all traces of strength, to differentiate it further from the effeminate form of her man. An appearance of strength in her body is called *ugly*.

Having projected her strength, her domestic component, onto the women beneath her, she achieves an image of frailty, weakness, helplessness, delicacy, daintiness. Silks, ruffles, frills, bangles, and laces are her element. In the realm of sex, because the act of sexual intercourse is both a physical and mental process, a joint venture between the Mind and the Body, her basic contradiction is that she is physically inadequate while mentally voracious, with her mind in extreme conflict with her body. The mechanism of her orgasm, which begins in her body and ends in the psychic depths of her mind, becomes short-circuited in the struggle between her mind and her body.

Sitting at the foot of her bed, like the mute Sphinx on the bank of the Nile, is the Ogre of Frigidity. She is terrified, because of the quality of her life, by the prospect of becoming a life-termer in the prison of frigidity. Her basic fear is frigidity, the state in which her frantic search for Ultrafemininity collides with an icepack death of the soul: where the fire in her body is extinguished by the ice in her mind. The psychic core of her sensuality, the male-seeking pole of her Female Principle, the trigger of the mechanism of her orgasm, moves beyond the reach or range of the effeminate clitoris of her man. Frigid, cold, icy, ice. Arctic. Antarctic. At the end of her flight from her body is a sky-high wall of ice. (If a lesbian is anything she is a frigid woman, a frozen cunt, with a warp and a crack in the wall of her ice.)

In proportion to the intensity of the Ultrafeminine's fear

and feel of the ice is her psychic lust for the flame, for the heat of the fire: the Body. The Ultrafeminine, seeking sexual satisfaction, finds only physical exhaustion in the bed of the Omnipotent Administrator, and the odds are against her finding psychic satisfaction there. Her "psychic bridegroom" is the Supermasculine Menial. The Omnipotent Administrator, having repudiated and abdicated his body, his masculine component which he has projected onto the men beneath him, cannot present his woman, the Ultrafeminine, with an image of masculinity capable of penetrating into the psychic depths where the treasure of her orgasm is buried. The sexual act being a joint venture of the Mind and Body, though he satisfy her body and sap its strength, he cannot touch that magic spot in her mind which triggers the mechanism of her orgasm. Bereft of psychic satisfaction, and inhibited by social conventions and mores from embarking on a quest for her sexual fulfillment, yet performing her function as a mother and wife to the Omnipotent Administrator, the Ultrafeminine becomes a psychic celibate.

At the nth degree of the Ultrafeminine's scale of psychic lust (the contours of which few men or women throughout their entire lives ever in fact explore, resort being had to the forms of sublimation) stands the walking phallus symbol of the Supermasculine Menial. Though she may never have had a sexual encounter with a Supermasculine Menial, she is fully convinced that he can fulfill her physical need. It will be no big thing for him to do since he can handle those Amazons down there with him, with his strong body, rippling muscles, his strength and fire, the driving force of his spine, the thrust of his hips and the fiery steel of his rod. But what wets the Ultrafeminine's juice is that she is allured and tortured by the secret, intuitive knowledge that he, her psychic bridegroom, can blaze through the wall of her ice, plumb her psychic depths, test the oil of her soul, melt the iceberg in her brain, touch her inner sanctum, detonate the bomb of her orgasm, and bring her sweet release.

The chip on the Supermasculine Menial's shoulder is the fact that he has been robbed of his mind. In an uncannily effective manner, the society in which he lives has assumed in its very structure that he, minus a mind, is the embodiment of Brute Power. The bias and reflex of the society are against the cultivation or even the functioning of his mind, and it is borne in upon him from all sides that the society is actually deaf, dumb, and blind to his mind. The products of his mind, unless they are very closely associated with his social function of Brute Power, are resented and held in contempt by society as a whole. The further away from Brute Power his mental productions stand, the more emphatically will they be rejected and scorned by society, and treated as upstart invasions of the realm of the Omnipotent Administrator. His thoughts count for nothing. He doesn't run, regulate, control, or administer anything. Indeed, he is himself regulated, manipulated, and controlled by the Omnipotent Administrators. The struggle of his life is for the emancipation of his mind, to receive recognition for the products of his mind, and official recognition of the fact that he has a mind.

In his society, the Mind has been adjudged superior to the Body, and he knows that he is the Body and the Omnipotent Administrator is the Mind. It's Mind over matter, and the Body is matter. He may despise the Omnipotent Administrator for his physical weakness and envy him for his mind; or he may despise his own body and idolize the weak body of the Omnipotent Administrator. He may even strive to attain a weak physical image himself in order to identify with the image of the Omnipotent Administrator. The people at the base of society, where the Supermasculine Menial is, are well known for their reflex of attempting to conform to the style, pattern, manners, and habits of the upper classes, of the Omnipotent Administrators and Ultrafeminines. Just how this works itself out is a problem for analysis by sociologists and social psychologists on the mass level, and the headshrinkers and nutcrackers on the individual level. What we are outlining here is a perspective from which such analysis might best be approached.

The psychic bride of the Supermasculine Menial is the Ultrafeminine. She is his "dream girl." She, the delicate, weak, helpless Ultrafeminine, exerts a magnetic attraction upon him. When he compares her with his own woman, the strong, self-reliant Amazon, lust for her burns in his brain. He recoils from the excess of strength injected into the Amazon by the Domestic Function she performs. Also, since standards of beauty are set by the elite, the Ultrafeminine personifies the official standard of feminine beauty of society as a whole. Influenced by and imbued with this official standard of beauty, while at the same time surrounded by Amazons who do not embody this standard and who are in fact clashing with it, the Supermasculine Menial develops an obsessive yearning and lust for sexual contact with the Ultrafeminine. These yearnings are compounded by the fact that on the whole they are foredoomed to remain unfulfilled. The society has arranged things so that the Supermasculine Menial and the Ultrafeminine are not likely to have access or propinquity to each other conducive to stimulating sexual involvement. In fact, it has not been rare for the Supermasculine Menial and the Ultrafeminine to be severely persecuted, if not put to death, for such sexual contact.

The Amazon is in a peculiar position. Just as her man has been deprived of his manhood, so she has been deprived of her full womanhood. Society has decreed that the Ultra-feminine, the woman of the elite, is the goddess on the pedestal. The Amazon is the personification of the rejected domestic component, the woman on whom "dishpan hands" seem not out of character. The worship and respect which both the Omnipotent Administrator and the Super-masculine Menial lavish upon the image of the Ultra-feminine is a source of deep vexation to the Amazon. She envies the pampered, powderpuff existence of the Ultra-feminine and longs to incorporate these elements into her own life. Alienated from the feminine component of her nature, her reinforced domestic component is an awesome burden and shame of which she longs to be free.

The Amazon finds it difficult to respect the Supermasculine Menial. She sees him essentially as only half a man, an incomplete man. Having no sovereignty over himself, he hasn't that sovereignty over her which our traditional patriarchal myths lead her to believe he should have. On a still deeper level, the urges and needs of the Amazon's psyche move her toward the source of power, toward the receptacle of sovereignty—an attraction motivated by the Primeval Urge to transcend the Primeval Mitosis. When the Primeval Sphere split into the male and female hemispheres, the attribute of sovereignty was reposited in the male hemisphere, and this attribute exercises a magnetic attraction upon the female hemisphere. Usurping the Super-masculine Menial's mind, the Omnipotent Administrator usurped all sovereignty; and because of his monopoly on sovereignty, he is the psychic bridegroom of the Amazon. In another sense, however, being also attracted to the body of the Supermasculine Menial, the Amazon is lost between two worlds.

In net effect, then, there will exist in Class Society two sets of competing images. Contending for the crown of masculinity is one image based on the Body and another based on the Mind; contending for the crown of femininity is one image based on weak, helpless Ultrafemininity and another based on the strong, self-reliant attributes of the Amazon. In a society with a racially homogeneous population, in which the people at the top are racially the same as the ones at the bottom, the competing images are not mutually exclusive. A Supermasculine Menial, for instance, who acquires the training of an Omnipotent Administrator, can become a member of the elite and function accordingly—assuming the existence of some vertical social mobility, which is not, of course, always the case. But even if he is prevented from ascending the social ladder in fact, a Supermasculine Menial can at least imagine himself doing so without first having to transcend any biological barriers. Likewise, an Omnipotent Administrator can descend the social ladder, develop his muscles, and hoe the row with the coolest serf on the manor. The women, too, can descend or ascend, depending on the merits, without having to breach a biological chain.

But in a society where there exists a racial caste system, where the people at the top are sharply distinguished from those at the bottom by race as well as social image, then the two sets of competing images can come to be considered mutually exclusive. The gulf between the Mind and the Body will seem to coincide with the gulf between the two races. At that point, the fear of biological miscegenation is transposed into social imagery; and since the distinction between the two races is founded in biology, the social distinction between Mind and Body is made sacred. Any attempt by the Supermasculine Menial to heal his wound and reclaim his mind will be viewed as a malignant desire to transcend the laws of nature by mixing, "mongrelizing," miscegenating. Coming from the other side, if a member of the elite should attempt to bridge the gulf, it will be conceived as the rankest form of degeneracy and treason to caste. Deep-seated fears and emotions, which are in fact connected with biological traits and are part of a mechanism to aid racial and ethnic survival, are harnessed to social images and thereby transformed into weapons of the Class Struggle. Race fears are weapons in the struggle between the Omnipotent Administrator and the Supermasculine Menial for control of sexual sovereignty.

The Supermasculine Menial and the Amazon are the least alienated from the biological chain, although their minds—especially the Supermasculine Menials'!—are in a general state of underdevelopment. Still, they are the wealth of a nation, an abundant supply of unexhausted, unde-essenced human raw material upon which the future of the society depends and with which, through the implacable march of history to an ever broader base of democracy and equality, the society will renew and transform itself.

Convalescence

. . . just as in childhood I envied Negroes for what seemed to me their superior masculinity, so I envy them today for what seems to me their superior physical grace and beauty. I have come to value physical grace very highly, and I am now capable of aching with all my being when I watch a Negro couple on the dance floor, or a Negro playing baseball or basketball. *They are on the kind of terms with their own bodies that I should like to be on with mine, and for that precious quality they seem blessed to me.* [Italics added]

—Norman Podhoretz,
"My Negro Problem—And Ours,"
Commentary, February 1963

Why envy the Negro his grace, his physical skills? Why not ask what it is that prevents grace and physical skill from becoming a general property of the young? Mr. Podhoretz speaks of middle-class, white respectability—what does this mean but being cut off from the labor process, the work process, the creative process, as such? *The solution is thus not the direct liquidation of the color line, through the liquidation of color; but rather through a greater physical connectedness of the whites; and a greater intellective connectedness of the blacks . . .*" [Italics added]

Irving Louis Horowitz, Chairman,
Department of Sociology, Hobart and William Smith Colleges,
Geneva, New York, *Commentary,* June 1963

If the separation of the black and white people in America along the color line had the effect, in terms of social imagery, of separating the Mind from the Body —the oppressor whites usurping sovereignty by monopolizing the Mind, abdicating the Body and becoming bodiless Omnipotent Administrators and Ultrafeminines; and the oppressed blacks, divested of sovereignty and therefore of Mind, manifesting the Body and becoming mindless Supermasculine Menials and Black Amazons—if this is so, then the 1954 U.S. Supreme Court decision in the case of *Brown* v. *Board of Education,* demolishing the principle of segregation of the races in public education and striking at the very root of the practice of segregation generally, was a major surgical operation performed by nine men in black robes on the racial Maginot Line which is imbedded as deep as sex or the lust for lucre in the schismatic American psyche. This piece of social surgery, if successful, performed without benefit of any anesthetic except God and the Constitution, in a land where God is dead and the Constitution has been in a coma for 180 years, is more marvelous than a successful heart transplant would be, for it was meant to graft the nation's Mind back onto its Body and vice versa.

If the foregoing is true, then the history of America in the years following the pivotal Supreme Court edict should be a record of the convalescence of the nation. And upon investigation we should be able to see the Omnipotent Administrators and Ultrafeminines grappling with their unfamiliar and alienated Bodies, and the Supermasculine Menials and Amazons attempting to acquire and assert *a mind of their own.* The record, I think, is clear and unequivocal. The bargain which seems to have been struck is that the whites have had to turn to the blacks for a clue on how to swing with the Body, while the blacks have had to turn to the whites for the secret of the Mind. It was Chubby Checker's mission, bearing the Twist as *good news,* to teach the whites, whom history had taught to forget, how to shake their asses again. It is a skill they surely must once have possessed but which they abandoned for puritanical dreams of escaping the corruption of the flesh, by leaving the terrors of the Body to the blacks.

In the swift, fierce years since the 1954 school desegregation decision, a rash of seemingly unrelated mass phenomena has appeared on the American scene—deviating radically from the prevailing Hot-Dog-and-Malted-Milk norm of the bloodless, square, superficial, faceless Sunday-Morning atmosphere that was suffocating the nation's soul. And all of this in a nation where the so-called molders of public opinion, the writers, politicians, teachers, and cab drivers, are willful, euphoric liars or zip-dam ostriches and owls, a clique of undercover ghosts, a bunch of Walter Jenkinses, a lot of coffee-drinking, cigarette-smoking, sly, suck-assing, status-seeking, cheating, nervous, dry-balled, tranquillizer-gulched, countdown-minded, out-of-style, slithering snakes. No wonder that many "innocent people," the manipulated and the stimulated, some of whom were game for a reasonable amount of mystery and even adventure, had their minds scrambled. These observers were not equipped to either *feel* or *know* that a radical break, a revolutionary leap out of their sight, had taken place in the secret parts of this nation's soul. It was as if a driverless vehicle were speeding through the American night down an unlighted street toward a stone wall and was boarded on the fly by a stealthy ghost with a drooling leer on his face, who, at the last detour before chaos and disaster, careened the vehicle down a smooth highway that leads to the future and life; and to ask these Americans to understand that they were the passengers on this driverless vehicle and that the lascivious ghost was the Saturday-night crotchfunk of the Twist, or the "Yeah, Yeah, Yeah!" which the Beatles high-jacked from Ray Charles, to ask these Calvinistic profligates to see the logical and reciprocal links is more cruel than asking a hope-to-die Okie Music buff to cop the sounds of John Coltrane.

In the beginning of the era came a thief with a seven-year itch who knew that the ostriches and the owls had been bribed with a fix of Euphony, which is their kick. The thief knew that he need not wait for the cover of night, that with impunity he could show his face in the marketplace in the full light of the sun, do his deed, scratch his dirt, sell his loot to the fence while the ostriches and owls, coasting on Euphony, one with his head in a hole—any hole—and the other with his head in the clouds, would only cluck and whisper and hear-see-speak no evil.

So Elvis Presley came, strumming a weird guitar and wagging his tail across the continent, ripping off fame and fortune as he scrunched his way, and, like a latter-day Johnny Appleseed, sowing seeds of a new rhythm and style in the white souls of the white youth of America, whose inner hunger and need was no longer satisfied with the antiseptic white shoes and whiter songs of Pat Boone. "You can do anything," sang Elvis to Pat Boone's white shoes, "but don't you step on my Blue Suede Shoes!"

During this period of ferment and beginnings, at about the same time that the blacks of Montgomery, Alabama, began their historic bus boycott (giving birth to the leadership of Martin Luther King, signifying to the nation that, with this initiative, this first affirmative step, somewhere in the universe a gear in the machinery had shifted), something, a target, came into focus. The tensions in the American psyche had torn a fissure in the racial Maginot Line and through this fissure, this tiny bridge between the Mind and Body, the black masses, who had been silent and somnolent since the '20s and '30s, were now making a break toward the dimly seen light that beckoned to them through the fissure. The fact that these blacks could now take such a step was perceived by the ostriches and owls as a sign of national decay, a sign that the System had caved in at that spot. And this gave birth to a fear, a fear that quickly became a focus for all the anxieties and exasperations in the Omnipotent Administrators' minds; and to embody this perceived decay and act as a lightning rod for the fear, the beatniks bloomed onto the American scene.

Like pioneers staking their claims in the no-man's land that lay along the racial Maginot Line, the beatniks, like Elvis Presley before them, dared to do in the light of day what America had long been doing in the sneak-thief anonymity of night—consorted on a human level with the blacks. Reviled, cursed, held in contempt by the "molders of public opinion," persecuted by the police, made into an epithet of derision by the deep-frozen geeks of the Hot-Dog-and-Malted-Milk set, the beatniks irreverently refused to go away. Allen Ginsberg and Jack Kerouac ("the Suzuki rhythm boys," James Baldwin called them, derisively, in a moment of panic, "tired of white ambitions" and "dragging themselves through the Negro street at dawn, looking for an angry fix"; "with," as Mailer put it, "the black man's code to fit their facts"). Bing Crosbyism, Perry Comoism, and Dinah Shoreism had led to cancer, and the vanguard of the white youth knew it.

And as the spirit of revolt crept across the continent from that wayward bus in Montgomery, Alabama, seeping like new life into the cracks and nooks of the northern ghettos and sweeping in furious gales across the campuses of southern Negro colleges, erupting, finally, in the sit-ins and freedom rides—as this swirling maelstrom of social change convulsed the nation, shocking an unsuspecting American public, folk music, speaking of fundamental verities, climbed slowly out of the grave; and the hip lobe of the national ear, twitching involuntarily at first, began to listen.

From the moment that Mrs. Rosa Parks, in that bus in Montgomery, Alabama, resisted the Omnipotent Administrator, contact, however fleeting, had been made with the lost sovereignty—the Body had made contact with its Mind—and the shock of that contact sent an electric current throughout this nation, traversing the racial Maginot Line and striking fire in the hearts of the whites. The wheels began to turn, the thaw set in, and though Emmett Till and Mack Parker were dead, though Eisenhower sent troops to Little Rock, though Autherine Lucy's token presence at the University of Alabama was a mockery—notwithstanding this, it was already clear that the 1954 major surgical operation had been successful and the patient would live. The challenge loomed on the horizon: Africa, black, enigmatic, and hard-driving, had begun to parade its newly freed nations into the UN; and the Islam of Elijah Muhammad, amplified as it was fired in salvos from the piercing tongue of Malcolm X, was racing through the Negro streets with Allen Ginsberg and Jack Kerouac.

Then, as the verbal revolt of the black masses soared to a cacophonous peak—the Body, the Black Amazons and Supermasculine Menials, becoming conscious, shouting, in a thousand different ways, *"I've got a Mind of my own!"* ; and as the senator from Massachusetts was saving the nation from the Strangelove grasp of Dirty Dick, injecting, as he emerged victorious, a new and vivacious spirit into the people with the style of his smile and his wife's hairdo; then, as if a signal had been given, as if the Mind had shouted to the Body, "I'm ready!"—the Twist, superseding the Hula Hoop, burst upon the scene like a nuclear explosion, sending its fallout of rhythm into the Minds and Bodies of the people. The fallout: the Hully Gully, the Mashed Potato, the Dog, the Smashed Banana, the Watusi, the Frug, the Swim. The Twist was a guided missile, launched from the ghetto into the very heart of suburbia. The Twist succeeded, as politics, religion, and law could never do, in writing in the heart and soul what the Supreme Court could only write on the books. The Twist was a form of therapy for a convalescing nation. The Omnipotent Administrator and the Ultrafeminine responded so dramatically, in stampede fashion, to the Twist precisely because it afforded them the possibility of reclaiming their Bodies again after generations of alienated and disembodied existence.

The stiff, mechanical Omnipotent Administrators and Ultrafeminines presented a startling spectacle as they entered in droves onto the dance floors to learn how to Twist. They came from every level of society, from top to bottom, writhing pitifully though gamely about the floor, feeling exhilarating and soothing new sensations, release from some unknown prison in which their Bodies had been encased, a sense of freedom they had never known before, a feeling of communion with some mystical root-source of life and vigor, from which sprang a new awareness and enjoyment of the flesh, a new appreciation of the possibilities of their Bodies. They were swinging and gyrating and shaking their dead little asses like petrified zombies trying to regain the warmth of life, rekindle the dead limbs, the cold ass, the stone heart, the stiff, mechanical, disused joints with the spark of life.

This spectacle truly startled many Negroes, because they perceived it as an intrusion by the Mind into the province of the Body, and this intimated chaos; because the Negroes knew, from the survival experience of their everyday lives, that the system within which they were imprisoned was based upon the racial Maginot Line and that the cardinal sin, crossing the line—which was, in their experience, usually initiated from the black side—was being committed, *en masse,* by the whites. The Omnipotent Administrators and Ultrafeminines were storming the Maginot Line! A massive assault had been launched without parallel in American history, and to Negroes it was confusing. Sure, they had witnessed it on an individual scale: they had seen many ofays destroy the Maginot Line in themselves. But this time it had all the appearances of a national movement. There were even rumors that President Kennedy and his Jackie were doing the Twist secretly in the White House; that their Number One Boy had been sent to the Peppermint Lounge in disguise to learn how to Twist, and he in turn brought the trick back to the White House. These Negroes knew that something fundamental had changed.

"Man, what done got into them ofays?" one asked.

"They trying to get back," said another.

"Shit," said a young Negro who made his living by shoplifting. "If you ask me, I think it must be the end of the world."

"Oooo-weee!" said a Negro musician who had been playing at a dance and was now standing back checking the dancers. "Baby, I don't dig this action at all! Look here, baby, pull my coat to what's going down! I mean, have I missed it somewhere? Where've I been? Baby, I been blowing all my life and I ain't never dug no happenings like this. You know what, man, I'm gon' cut that fucking weed aloose. Oooo-weee! Check that little bitch right there! What the fuck she trying to do? Is she trying to shake it or break it? Oooo-weee!"

A Negro girl said: "Take me home, I'm sick!"

Another one said: "No, let's stay! This is too much!"

And a bearded Negro cat, who was not interested in learning how to Twist himself, who felt that if he was interested in doing it, he could get up from the table right now and start Twisting, he said, sitting at the table with a tinsel-minded female: "It ain't nothing. They just trying to get back, that's all."

"Get back?" said the girl, arching her brows quizzically, "Get back from where?"

"From wherever they've been," said the cat, "where else?"

"Are they doing it in Mississippi is what I want to know," said a tall, deadly looking Negro who had a long razor line down his left cheek and who had left Mississippi in a hurry one night.

And the dancers: they were caught up in a whirl of ecstasy, swinging like pendulums, mechanical like metronomes or puppets on invisible strings being manipulated by a master with a sick sense of humor. "They look like Chinese doing communal exercise," said a Negro. "That's all they're doing, calisthenics!"

"Yeah," said his companion. "They're trying to get in shape."

But if at first it was funny and confusing, it was nonetheless a breakthrough. The Omnipotent Administrators and Ultrafeminines were discovering new aspects of the Body, new possibilities of rhythm, new ways to move. The Hula Hoop had been a false start, a mechanized, theatrical attempt by the Mind to supply to itself what only the Body can give. But, with the Twist, at last they knew themselves to be swinging. The forces acting upon the world stage in our era had created, in the collective psyche of the Omnipotent Administrators and Ultrafeminines, an irresistible urge—to just stand up and shake the ice and cancer out of their alienated white asses—and the Hula Hoop and Twist offered socially acceptable ways to do it.

Of course, not all the whites took part in these joyful experiments. For many, the more "suggestive" a dance became—i.e., the more it became pure Body and less Mind—the more scandalous it seemed to them; and their reaction in this sense was an index to the degree of their alienation from their Bodies. But what they condemned as a sign of degeneracy and moral decay was actually a sign of health, a sign of hope for full recovery. As Norman Mailer prophesied: ". . . the Negro's equality would tear a profound shift into the psychology, the sexuality, and the moral imagination of every white alive." Precisely because the Mind will have united with the Body, theory will have merged with practice.

It is significant that the Twist and the Hula Hoop came into the scene in all their fury at the close of the Eisenhower and the dawn of the Kennedy era. It could be interpreted as a rebellion against the vacuous Eisenhower years. It could also be argued that the same collective urge that gave rise to the Twist also swept Kennedy into office. I shudder to think that, given the closeness of the final vote in 1960, Richard Nixon might have won the election in a breeze if he had persuaded one of his Ultrafeminine daughters, not to mention Ultrapat, to do the Twist in public. Not if Kennedy had stayed on the phone a week sympathizing with Mrs. Martin Luther King, Jr., over the fact that the cat was in jail, would he have won. Even as I am convinced that Luci Baines Johnson, dancing the Watusi in public with Killer Joe Piro, won more votes for her old man in 1964 than a whole boxcar full of his hog-calling speeches ever did.

When the Birmingham Revolt erupted in the summer of 1963 and President Kennedy stepped into the void and delivered his unprecedented speech to the nation on civil rights and sent his bill to Congress, the foundation had been completed. Martin Luther King, Jr., giving voice to the needs of the Body, and President Kennedy, speaking out the needs of the Mind, made contact on that day. The Twisters, sporting their blue suede shoes, moved beyond the ghost in white shoes who ate a Hot Dog and sipped Malted Milk as he danced the mechanical jig of Satan on top of Medgar Evers' tomb. In vain now would the murderers bomb that church and slaughter grotesquely those four little black girls (what did they hope to kill? were they striking at the black of the skin or the fire of the soul? at history? at the Body?). In vain also the assassins' bullets that crashed through the head of John Kennedy, taking a life, yes, but creating a larger-than-life and failing utterly to expunge from the record the March on Washington and its truth: that this nation—bourgeois or not, imperialist or not, murderous or not, ugly or not—its people, somewhere in their butchered and hypocritical souls, still contained an epic potential of spirit which is its hope, a bottomless potential which fires the imaginations of its youth. It was all too late. It was too late because it was time for the blacks ("I've got a *Mind* of my own!") to riot, to sweep through the Harlem night like a wave of locusts, breaking, screaming, bleeding, laughing, crying, rejoicing, celebrating, in a jubilee of destruction, to regurgitate the white man's bullshit they'd been eating for four hundred years; smashing the windows of the white man's stores, throwing bricks they wished were bombs, running, leaping whirling like a cyclone through the white man's Mind, past his backlash, through the night streets of Rochester, New Jersey, Philadelphia. And even though the opposition, gorging on Hot Dogs and Malted Milk, with blood now splattered over the white shoes, would still strike out in the dark against the manifestations of the turning, showing the protocol of

Southern Hospitality reserved for Niggers and Nigger Lovers
—*SCHWERNER–CHANEY–GOODMAN*—it was still
too late. For not only had Luci Baines Johnson danced
the Watusi in public with Killer Joe, but the Beatles
were on the scene, injecting Negritude by the ton into the
whites, in this post–Elvis Presley-beatnik era of ferment.

Before we toss the Beatles a homosexual kiss—saying,
"If a man be ass enough to reach for the bitch in them, that
man will kiss a man, and if a woman reaches for the stud in
them, that woman will kiss a woman"—let us marvel at the
genius of their image, which comforts the owls and ostriches in the one spot where Elvis Presley bummed their
kick: Elvis, with his *un*funky (yet mechanical, alienated)
bumpgrinding, was still too much Body (too soon) for the
strained collapsing psyches of the Omnipotent Administrators and Ultrafeminines; whereas the Beatles, affecting
the caucasoid crown of femininity and ignoring the Body
on the visual plane (while their music on the contrary being
full of Body), assuaged the doubts of the owls and ostriches
by presenting an incorporeal, cerebral image.

Song and dance are, perhaps, only a little less old than
man himself. It is with his music and dance, the recreation
through art of the rhythms suggested by and implicit in the
tempo of his life and cultural environment, that man purges
his soul of the tensions of daily strife and maintains his
harmony in the universe. In the increasingly mechanized,
automated, cybernated environment of the modern world
—a cold, bodiless world of wheels, smooth plastic surfaces,
tubes, pushbuttons, transistors, computers, jet propulsion,
rockets to the moon, atomic energy—man's need for affirmation of his biology has become that much more intense.
He feels need for a clear definition of where his body ends
and the machine begins, where man ends and the *extensions*
of man begin. This great mass hunger, which transcends

national or racial boundaries, recoils from the subtle sub-
versions of the mechanical environment which modern
technology is creating faster than man, with his present
savage relationship to his fellow men, is able to receive and
assimilate. This is the central contradiction of the twentieth
century; and it is against this backdrop that America's
attempt to unite its Mind with its Body, to save its soul, is
taking place.

It is in this connection that the blacks, personifying the
Body and thereby in closer communion with their biological roots than other Americans, provide the saving link, the
bridge between man's biology and man's machines. In its
purest form, as adjustment to the scientific and technologi-
cal environment of our era, as purgative and lullaby-
soother of man's soul, it is the jazz issuing from the friction
and harmony of the American Negro with his environment
that captured the beat and tempo of our times. And although modern science and technology are the same
whether in New York, Paris, London, Accra, Cairo, Berlin,
Moscow, Tokyo, Peking, or São Paulo, jazz is the only true
international medium of communication current in the
world today, capable of speaking creatively, with equal
intensity and relevance, to the people in all those places.

The less sophisticated (but no less Body-based) popular
music of urban Negroes—which was known as Rhythm and
Blues before the whites appropriated and distilled it into a
product they called Rock 'n Roll—is the basic ingredient,
the core, of the gaudy, cacophonous hymns with which the
Beatles of Liverpool drive their hordes of Ultrafeminine
fans into catatonia and hysteria. For Beatle fans, having
been alienated from their own Bodies so long and so
deeply, the effect of these potent, erotic rhythms is electric.
Into this music, the Negro projected—as it were, *drained
off*, as pus from a sore—a powerful sensuality, his pain and

lust, his love and his hate, his ambition and his despair. The Negro projected into his music his very Body. The Beatles, the four long-haired lads from Liverpool, are offering up as their gift the Negro's Body, and in so doing establish a rhythmic communication between the listener's own Mind and Body.

Enter the Beatles—soul by proxy, middlemen between the Mind and the Body. A long way from Pat Boone's White Shoes. A way station on a slow route traveled with all deliberate speed.

To All Black Women,
From All Black Men

Queen–Mother–Daughter of Africa
Sister of My Soul
Black Bride of My Passion
My Eternal Love

I greet you, my Queen, not in the obsequious whine of a cringing Slave to which you have become accustomed, neither do I greet you in the new voice, the unctuous supplications of the sleek Black Bourgeoise, nor the bullying bellow of the rude Free Slave—but in my own voice do I greet you, the voice of the Black Man. And although I greet you *anew*, my greeting is not *new*, but as old as the Sun, Moon, and Stars. And rather than mark a new beginning, my greeting signifies only my Return.

I have Returned from the dead. I speak to you now from the Here And Now. I was dead for four hundred years. For four hundred years you have been a woman alone, bereft of her man, a manless woman. For four hundred years I was neither your man nor my own man. The white man stood between us, over us, around us. The white man was your man and my man. Do not pass lightly over this truth, my Queen, for even though the fact of it has burned into the marrow of our bones and diluted our blood, we must bring

205

it to the surface of the mind, into the realm of knowing, glue our gaze upon it and stare at it as at a coiled serpent in a baby's playpen or the fresh flowers on a mother's grave. It is to be pondered and realized in the heart, for the heel of the white man's boot is our point of departure, our point of Resolve and Return—the bloodstained pivot of our future. (But I would ask you to recall, that before we could come up from slavery, we had to be pulled down from our throne.)

Across the naked abyss of negated masculinity, of four hundred years minus my Balls, we face each other today, my Queen. I feel a deep, terrifying hurt, the pain of humiliation of the vanquished warrior. The shame of the fleet-footed sprinter who stumbles at the start of the race. I feel unjustified. I can't bear to look into your eyes. Don't you know (surely you must have noticed by now: four hundred years!) that for four hundred years I have been unable to look squarely into your eyes? I tremble inside each time you look at me. I can feel . . . in the ray of your eye, from a deep hiding place, a long-kept secret you harbor. That is the unadorned truth. Not that I would have felt justified, under the circumstances, in taking such liberties with you, but I want you to know that I feared to look into your eyes because I knew I would find reflected there a merciless Indictment of my impotence and a compelling challenge to redeem my conquered manhood.

My Queen, it is hard for me to tell you what is in my heart for you today—what is in the heart of all my black brothers for you and all your black sisters—and I fear I will fail unless you reach out to me, tune in on me with the antenna of your love, the sacred love in ultimate degree which you were unable to give me because I, being dead, was unworthy to receive it; that perfect, radical love of black on which our Fathers thrived. Let me drink from the river of your love at its source, let the lines of force of your love seize my soul by its core and heal the wound of my Castration, let my convex exile end its haunted Odyssey in your concave essence which receives that it may give. Flower of Africa, it is only through the liberating power of your *re*-love that my manhood can be redeemed. For it is in your eyes, before you, that my need is to be justified, Only, only, only you and only you can condemn or set me free.

Be convinced, Sable Sister, that the past is no forbidden vista upon which we dare not look, out of a phantom fear of being, as the wife of Lot, turned into pillars of salt. Rather the past is an omniscient mirror: we gaze and see reflected there ourselves and each other—what we used to be, what we are today, how we got this way, and what we are becoming. To decline to look into the Mirror of Then, my heart, is to refuse to view the face of Now.

I have died the ninth death of the cat, have seen Satan face to face and turned my back on God, have dined in the Swine's Trough, and descended to the uttermost echelon of the Pit, have entered the Den and seized my Balls from the teeth of a roaring lion!

Black Beauty, in impotent silence I listened, as if to a symphony of sorrows, to your screams for help, anguished pleas of terror that echo still throughout the Universe and through the mind, a million scattered screams across the painful years that merged into a single sound of pain to haunt and bleed the soul, a white-hot sound to char the brain and blow the fuse of thought, a sound of fangs and teeth sharp to eat the heart, a sound of moving fire, a sound of frozen heat, a sound of licking flames, a fiery-fiery sound, a sound of fire to burn the steel out of my Balls, a sound of

Blue fire, a Bluesy sound, the sound of dying, the sound of my woman in pain, *the sound of my woman's pain,* THE SOUND OF MY WOMAN CALLING ME, ME, I HEARD HER CALL FOR HELP, I HEARD THAT MOURNFUL SOUND BUT HUNG MY HEAD AND FAILED TO HEED IT, I HEARD MY WOMAN'S CRY, I HEARD MY WOMAN'S SCREAM, I HEARD MY WOMAN BEG THE BEAST FOR MERCY, I HEARD HER BEG FOR ME, I HEARD MY WOMAN BEG THE BEAST FOR MERCY FOR ME, I HEARD MY WOMAN DIE, I HEARD THE SOUND OF HER DEATH, A SNAPPING SOUND, A BREAKING SOUND, A SOUND THAT SOUNDED FINAL, THE LAST SOUND, THE ULTIMATE SOUND, THE SOUND OF DEATH, ME, I HEARD, I HEAR IT EVERY DAY, I HEAR HER NOW . . . I HEAR YOU NOW . . . I HEAR YOU.

. . . I heard you then . . . your scream came like a searing bolt of lightning that blazed a white streak down my black back. In a cowardly stupor, with a palpitating heart and quivering knees, I watched the Slaver's lash of death slash through the opposing air and bite with teeth of fire into your delicate flesh, the black and tender flesh of African Motherhood, forcing the startled Life untimely from your torn and outraged womb, the sacred womb that cradled primal man, the womb that incubated Ethiopia and populated Nubia and gave forth Pharaohs unto Egypt, the womb that painted the Congo black and mothered Zulu, the womb of Mero, the womb of the Nile, of the Niger, the womb of Songhay, of Mali, of Ghana, the womb that felt the might of Chaka before he saw the Sun, the Holy Womb, the womb that knew the future form of Jomo Kenyatta, the womb of Mau Mau, the womb of the blacks, the womb that nurtured Toussaint L'Ouverture, that warmed Nat Turner, and Gabriel Prosser, and Denmark Vesey, the black womb that surrendered up in tears that nameless and endless chain of Africa's Cream, the Black Cream of the Earth, that nameless and endless black chain that sank in heavy groans into oblivion in the great abyss, the womb that received and nourished and held firm the seed and gave back Sojourner Truth, and Sister Tubman, and Rosa Parks, and Bird, and Richard Wright, and your other works of art who wore and wear such names as Marcus Garvey and DuBois and Kwame Nkrumah and Paul Robeson and Malcolm X and Robert Williams, and the one you bore in pain and called Elijah Muhammad, but most of all that nameless one they tore out of your womb in a flood of murdered blood that splashed upon and seeped into the mud. And Patrice Lumumba, and Emmett Till, and Mack Parker.

O, My Soul! I became a sniveling craven, a funky punk, a vile, groveling bootlicker, with my will to oppose petrified by a cosmic fear of the Slavemaster. Instead of inciting the Slaves to rebellion with eloquent oratory, I soothed their hurt and eloquently sang the Blues! Instead of hurling my life with contempt into the face of my Tormentor, *I shed your precious blood!* When Nat Turner sought to free me from my Fear, my Fear delivered him up unto the Butcher —a martyred monument to my Emasculation. My spirit was unwilling and my flesh was weak. Ah, eternal ignominy!

I, the Black Eunuch, divested of my Balls, walked the earth with my mind locked in Cold Storage. I would kill a black man or woman quicker than I'd smash a fly, while for the white man I would pick a thousand pounds of cotton a day. What profit is there in the blind, frenzied efforts of the (Guilty!) Black Eunuchs (Justifiers!) who hide their wounds and scorn the truth to mitigate their culpability through the pallid sophistry of postulating a Universal Democracy of Cowards, pointing out that in history no one can hide, that if not at one time then surely at another the iron heel of the Conqueror has ground into the mud the

Balls of Everyman? Memories of yesterday will not assuage the torrents of blood that flow today from my crotch. Yes, History could pass for a scarlet text, its jot and tittle graven red in human blood. More armies than shown in the books have planted flags on foreign soil leaving Castration in their wake. But no Slave should die a natural death. There is a point where Caution ends and Cowardice begins. Give me a bullet through the brain from the gun of the beleaguered oppressor on the night of seige. Why is there dancing and singing in the Slave Quarters? A Slave who dies of natural causes cannot balance two dead flies in the Scales of Eternity. Such a one deserves rather to be pitied than mourned.

Black woman, without asking how, just say that we survived our forced march and travail through the Valley of Slavery, Suffering, and Death—there, that Valley there beneath us hidden by that drifting mist. Ah, what sights and sounds and pain lie beneath that mist! And we had thought that our hard climb out of that cruel valley led to some cool, green and peaceful, sunlit place—but it's all jungle here, a wild and savage wilderness that's overrun with ruins.

But put on your crown, my Queen, and we will build a New City on these ruins.